ANCIENT TECHNOLOGY

ANCIENT AGRICULTURE

ANCIENT TECHNOLOGY

ANCIENT AGRICULTURE

FROM FORAGING TO FARMING

by Michael Woods

and

Mary B. Woods

RP RUNESTONE PRESS · MINNEAPOLIS

A DIVISION OF LERNER PUBLISHING GROUP

Dedicated to Jeremy, Matthew, Cathleen, and Margaret

Copyright © 2000 by Michael Woods and Mary B. Woods

Series designer: Zachary Marell
Series editors: Joelle E. Riley and Dina Drits
Line editor: Margaret J. Goldstein
Photograph researcher: Dan Mahoney

Runestone Press
A Division of Lerner Publishing Group
241 First Avenue North
Minneapolis, MN 55401 U.S.A.

Website address: www.lernerbooks.com

LIBRARY OF CONGRESS CATALOGING-IN-PUBLICATION DATA

Woods, Michael, 1946–
    Ancient agriculture : from foraging to farming / by Michael Woods and Mary B. Woods.
        p.   cm. — (Ancient technology)
    Includes bibliographical references (p.   ) and index.
    Summary: Discusses agricultural technology in various cultures from the Stone Age to A.D. 476, including China, Egypt, Mesoamerica, and Greece.
    ISBN 0-8225-2995-5 (alk. paper)
    1. Agriculture—History—Juvenile literature. 2. Agriculture—origin—Juvenile literature. [1. Agriculture—History.]
 I. Woods, Mary B. (Mary Boyle), 1946–. II. Title. III. Series.
    S421.W66 2000
    630'.9'01—dc21   98-48497

Manufactured in the United States of America
1 2 3 4 5 6 – AM – 05 04 03 02 01 00

TABLE OF CONTENTS

What do you think of when you hear the word *technology?* You probably think of something totally new. You might think of research laboratories filled with computers, powerful microscopes, and other scientific tools. But technology doesn't refer only to brand-new machines and discoveries. Technology is as old as human society.

Technology is the use of knowledge, inventions, and discoveries to make life better. The word *technology* comes from two Greek words. One, *tekhne*, means "art" or "craft." The other, *logos*, means "word" or "speech." Ancient Greeks originally used the word to mean a discussion of arts and crafts. But, in modern times, *technology* usually refers to an art, tool, or technique itself.

People use many kinds of technology. Medicine is one kind of technology. Transportation and machinery are also kinds of technology. These technologies and many others help make human life easier, safer, and more enjoyable. This book looks at a form of technology that has changed human life more than any other: agriculture.

Agriculture is the production of plants and animals useful to humans. Agricultural technology includes raising crops, breeding and managing livestock, and preparing and preserving plant and animal products.

The story of agriculture is the story of human civilization. Civilizations are settled societies with systems of government, religion, social class, labor, and record keeping. Without agriculture, humans would not have settled in towns and cities. We would still be hunter-gatherers, roaming from place to place finding food. There would be no civilization.

ANCIENT ROOTS

You've probably heard people remark, "There's nothing new under the sun!" That's especially true when we're talking about agriculture and food production. Fifteen crops provide about 80 percent of the world's food supply, and most of them were domesticated in ancient times. Ancient people also developed most of our basic technologies for food preservation.

An ancient Greek or Roman somehow transported to modern times would marvel at the output of modern farms and the assortment of modern foods. But he or she might also be amazed at how little some basic farming technologies have changed over the centuries.

The word *ancient* refers to the period of time from the emergence of the first humans on earth to the fall of the Western Roman Empire in A.D. 476. The first human beings lived about 2.5 million years ago.

Use of technology is one trait that archaeologists—scientists who study the remains of past societies—use to distinguish human beings from their prehuman ancestors. Early people used sharp sticks to dig furrows for planting seeds. Those sticks were the first agricultural tools.

NORTH
AMERICA

Atlantic
Ocean

Pacific
Ocean

N

SOUTH
AMERICA

CIVILIZATIONS OF THE
Ancient World
(through A.D. 476)

EUROPE

ASIA

AFRICA

Indian
Ocean

6000 B.C. ——————————— 534 B.C.		Middle East
3100 B.C. ——————— 30 B.C.		Egypt
1766 B.C. ————————————		China
1200 B.C. ————————————		Mesoamerica
800 B.C. ——— 146 B.C.		Greece
509 B.C. —— A.D. 476		Rome
320 B.C. ——		India

Stone Age civilizations have flourished in
most parts of the world. These cultures began and
ended at different times in different regions.

The technology was primitive, but it was effective.

Some textbooks say that agriculture started about ten thousand years ago in the Fertile Crescent, an area in the ancient Middle East. The Fertile Crescent extended from the Persian Gulf through the valleys of the Tigris and Euphrates Rivers to Egypt. Some of the world's first agricultural societies began there. But the Fertile Crescent was not the only place were people began to farm. There were also farmers in ancient China, Mexico, South America, and other places.

In some areas, crops and agricultural technology spread as ancient countries conquered and traded with one another. In other instances, agricultural technology developed in isolation.

A LOT WITH A LITTLE

Ancient farmers did not have motorized equipment to work the soil and harvest crops. There were no assembly lines for processing and preserving food. Yet ancient people domesticated almost all of the plants and animals that we still depend on for food. They developed methods for making bread, cheese, wine, beer, olive oil, and other basic foods.

Ancient people left us a rich legacy of agricultural technology. This book tells the story of this technology. Be prepared for surprises and lots of fun. After all, ancient people ate some unusual foods. They used strange recipes. They were true agricultural scientists who were not afraid to experiment. Read on and discover the history of many of your favorite foods.

THE STONE AGE

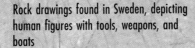

Rock drawings found in Sweden, depicting human figures with tools, weapons, and boats

The Stone Age began with the first humans on earth. Archaeologists often divide the Stone Age into two parts. The Old Stone Age, or Paleolithic period, began more than two million years ago and lasted until about 10,000 B.C. The New Stone Age, or Neolithic period, lasted from about 10,000 B.C. to about 3500 B.C. Archaeologists have found remains of Stone Age cultures in China, Africa, Europe, Asia, the Middle East, and other parts of the world.

Stone Age people were hunters and gatherers. They lived by fishing, catching game, and gathering wild, edible plants such as nuts, acorns, grains, berries, and fruits. After eating the food in one area, people moved on to another place with more food. Sometimes they followed herds of wild animals, which were also a source of food.

Stone Age people were also scavengers. They competed with vultures and hyenas for scraps of meat on animal bones left by lions and other predators. People probably used stones to crack animal bones and get at the tasty marrow inside. Some evidence suggests that humans used fire to cook meat as early as 400,000 B.C.

Human beings changed over time, becoming smarter and more skillful. Modern human beings, *Homo sapiens*, emerged more than 90,000 years ago. They were skilled hunters and gatherers. They had bigger and more capable brains than earlier types of humans. They developed better stone and bone tools for hunting. They knew how to kill large, elephantlike mammoths and butcher them with razor-sharp stone knives.

Stone Age people probably were not searching for the most tasty foods. They were just trying to find enough food to survive. They devoted almost every waking hour to the search for food. When drought, wildfire, disease, or other natural disasters reduced the supply of food, people starved and died. The constant quest for food made it difficult for Stone Age people to develop better technology and true civilization.

ANCIENT FISH FRIES

Stone Age people did enjoy a variety of foods, though. Fish and shellfish were a major source of food. Archaeologists have found fossilized fish bones at camps where people ate 380,000 years ago. Trash heaps at 100,000-year-old campsites contain so many fish bones that archaeologists believe that fishing was common in the Stone Age.

What kinds of fish did Stone Age people like best? Many of the same fish that modern people favor. Fossilized fish bones and paintings made by Stone Age cave dwellers show that salmon was the most popular seafood, followed by trout, perch, pike, and eel.

SPEARS AND TRAPS

Stone Age people sometimes caught fish by hand. But they also used spears, nets, and other traps. Remains of some of the world's oldest fishing nets, made from vines and dating to 7500 B.C., have been discovered in northern Europe.

The Magdalenian people, who lived in France around 13,000 B.C., used barbed spears for fishing. The spears had sharpened points that curved backward to keep fish from slipping away. Barbs were made from animal bone or antler.

Ancient people also built weirs, fencelike structures made out of vines, piles of tree branches, or sticks pounded closely together in streambeds. The current swept fish into these traps.

FISHHOOKS

The first fishhook was made about 25,000 years ago. The hook consisted of a short sharp stick, or toggle, tied to a vine and baited with a worm or insect. When a fish snapped at the bait, the toggle wedged in the fish's mouth. The Stone Age angler then hauled in a tasty meal.

About 10,000 years ago in the Middle East and Egypt, people began to make fishhooks from curved pieces of wood, bone, and oyster shell. The greatest advance in fishhook technology was the introduction of the barb. Unbarbed hooks worked only when they happened to wedge in a fish's mouth or gills. Hooks often slipped out when an angler pulled on a line to haul in a catch. Barbed hooks were much more efficient. They stuck firmly in place, even

Fish fossil found at Monte Bolca, Italy

with a lot of tension on the fishing line. The first metal fishhooks were made from copper, by the Boian people of ancient Germany around 3800 B.C.

FOOD PRESERVATION

Many modern people eat smoked, dried, or salted fish. In ancient times, smoking, drying, and salting were the only ways of preventing fish and meat from spoiling in warm weather. Recipes used five thousand years ago in ancient Babylon call for crumbling dried fish paste into soups and stews.

But food preservation is much more ancient than that. Studies of fossilized fish bones indicate that people preserved fish during the Paleolithic age by smoking it. The discovery probably happened by chance, when people observed that fish exposed to smoky campfires and coated with smoke particles lasted longer than fish that hadn't been smoked.

STONE AGE REFRIGERATORS

Ancient hunters living in North America faced a big problem after killing mastodons. Mastodons, extinct relatives of modern elephants, yielded hundreds of pounds of meat— far too much for hunters and their families to eat at once. How did Stone Age people keep this meat from spoiling?

They probably recognized that cold temperatures could prevent food spoilage. Daniel C. Fisher, a professor at the University of Michigan, thinks that Stone Age people refrigerated meat. No, they did not use electric refrigerators or freezers. They used a technology called underwater caching. This involves sinking chunks of meat into lakes and ponds, where cold water, bacteria, and low levels of oxygen keep the meat from rotting. Dr. Fisher discovered evidence of underwater caching while excavating 11,000-year-old butchered mastodons in Michigan, Ohio, Indiana, and New York.

Could underwater caching really keep meat fresh enough to eat months after a kill? Scientists who study prehistory sometimes try to answer such questions by re-creating ancient technology. So Dr. Fisher and two coworkers performed an experiment. One autumn, they anchored pieces of lamb, deer, and horse meat in the bottom of a pond. They also stored control, or comparison, samples in a modern freezer. They periodically tested samples in a laboratory. After six months, the researchers found the cached meat was just as well preserved as the meat stored in the freezer.

After hot weather arrived in June, the underwater caches of meat developed a strong odor and a sour taste. But tests showed that the meat was still nourishing. Dr. Fisher's recreation of ancient technology showed that early residents of North America could have preserved mastodon meat for months.

THE GOLDEN AGE OF NUTRITION

Some experts say it was the Stone Age! In 1988, three scientists published a book called *The Paleolithic Prescription.* The book urged people to take a nutrition, or diet, lesson from their ancestors who lived 40,000 years ago. The authors of the book concluded that hunter-gatherers ate the perfect diet, with just the right balance of meat, vegetables, and fat.

The typical Paleolithic person ate a diet that was about 65 percent vegetables and 35 percent meat. The meat was low in fat and cholesterol because it came from wild animals rather than fattened domestic ones. The Paleolithic diet also was high in fiber—plant material that has health benefits. Stone Age people ate almost no sugar and very little salt. They had massive bones and were almost four inches taller, on average, than people in the first agricultural societies.

Some health experts want modern people to return to a Stone Age diet. They believe it could reduce illness and death from heart disease, cancer, and other conditions.

Stone Age Sweets

About 12,000 years ago, a Paleolithic artist in the Cave of the Spider near the modern Spanish city of Valencia drew an exciting scene. It shows a man clinging to long vines or ropes and reaching into a cavity in the cave wall itself. The man is collecting something and putting it into a woven basket grasped in his other hand.

What do you think he was collecting? Here's a clue: The picture shows a swarm of little dots emerging from the cavity and surrounding the man. The man was collecting honey, and the dots were bees determined to protect their own treasure.

Similar scenes appear in caves in many other parts of the world, suggesting that people in many ancient societies used honey. Honey was a food and medicine in ancient times. Sometimes it was mixed with water and fermented to produce an alcoholic beverage called mead.

A Changing Society

Ancient people changed from hunters and gatherers to farmers when they began to domesticate wild plants and animals. Domesticate means to change, and perhaps improve, a wild species for human use.

At first, ancient people probably domesticated plants and animals without planning to do it. Farmers then made a deliberate effort to breed domestic animals. Generations of such breeding changed the very nature of animals, so that domestic animals were physically different from their wild counterparts.

Throughout the world, ancient farmers domesticated more than 20 wild animals, including the dog, sheep, goat, pig, cow, guinea pig, silkworm moth, llama, ass, camel, horse, honeybee, water buffalo, duck, yak, chicken, cat, goose, alpaca, and reindeer. Plants were domesticated and improved with much the same kind of breeding.

When ancient people domesticated plants and animals, they also domesticated themselves. Agriculture freed people from the need to spend every waking hour searching for food. With the extra time, people could build villages and cities; create literature, laws, and works of art; and invent new forms of technology to improve their lives.

With a reliable food source, people were healthier and lived longer. More children survived to adulthood. With the start of agriculture, the earth's population nearly doubled, from less than 3 million people in 10,000 B.C. to 5.3 million in 8000 B.C. Historians often refer to this advancement as the "agricultural revolution."

DOMESTICATING ANIMALS

Archaeologists think that dogs—which were domesticated from wolves—were the first domestic animals. People and dogs probably became companions in the Paleolithic period. Hunters probably brought wolf cubs back to camp after killing the parents for their warm skins. Then the humans raised the cubs. After many generations, the animals became tamer and more like modern dogs.

Pet dogs protected Stone Age people and helped in hunting. Dogs scared away enemies, killed snakes, and kept

Egyptian stone carving of hunters with dogs and deer

mice and rats from eating stored food. Cave paintings in many parts of the world show dogs in such roles. One of the oldest known dog skeletons dates to 8500 B.C. and was found in Idaho.

ANCIENT MIDDLE EAST

Eighth century B.C. tablet showing cooks at a royal stable in Assyria

The earth has gone through many ice ages, long periods of cold temperatures when much of the land was covered with sheets of ice. The most recent ice age ended around 11,000 B.C.

In the ancient Middle East, as the last ice age came to an end and the earth grew warmer, enormous fields of wild wheat, barley, and other grains began to grow in the warm temperatures. The grain reseeded itself and grew year after year.

Gradually, Stone Age hunter-gatherers began to rely on the wild grain for food. Slowly, their wandering lifestyle began to change. They built villages and began growing grain and domesticating nearby wild animals.

Civilizations began to emerge throughout the Middle East, in the region known as the Fertile Crescent. The Sumerians were one of several groups living in Mesopotamia, between the Tigris and Euphrates Rivers, in present-day

Iraq. Other groups in the ancient Middle East included the Assyrians, Babylonians, and Phoenicians.

These Middle Eastern civilizations developed many foods and food production technologies. They were the first people to domesticate wheat. They also domesticated many animals. They developed methods for making bread, olive oil, wine, beer, and cheese.

Advances in agriculture helped to inspire other kinds of technology. To record land boundaries and the size of goat herds, for instance, Middle Eastern farmers developed a form of writing. To make clay pots and jars for storing grain, goat's milk, and other agricultural products, Middle Eastern farmers invented the potter's wheel. That device may have been the model for the greatest of all transportation technologies—the wheel.

GOATS AND SHEEP

Wild goats and sheep were abundant in the hills of the Middle East. Some archaeologists believe that early hunters brought back baby sheep and goats as family pets after killing the adult animals. Next, people began keeping the animals for milk and meat.

Sheep and goats have strong herding instincts. They tend to stay together in groups and follow lead animals. So it was easy for early farmers to keep the animals from running away. Baby sheep and goats also undergo "imprinting": they form a strong bond with their mothers. But if the mother is killed or taken away soon after a baby animal's birth, the baby will bond to, and follow, a human. For these reasons, ancient Middle Easterners were able to tame sheep and goats quite easily.

Babylonian clay tablet with cuneiform writing listing the dimensions of fields

Next, ancient farmers learned to breed animals with desirable traits. If a farmer wanted big, even-tempered sheep that gave lots of milk, he mated animals with those characteristics. Sheep that were small, bad tempered, or poor milk producers were butchered for meat. Eventually, the farmer's herds consisted mainly of large, docile sheep that gave lots of milk.

TECHNOLOGY BREEDS TECHNOLOGY

Sometimes, one technological advance creates the need for another. Here's an example. The Phoenicians made a beautiful purple dye, named Tyrian purple for the Phoenician seaport of Tyre. The dye came from a shellfish, *Murex brandaris*. Rare and costly, Tyrian purple became a symbol of royalty and wealth in the ancient world. Kings and emperors wore clothing made from wool that had been dyed purple. An emperor who was the son of an emperor was said to be *porphyriogenatos*—"born to the purple."

Archaeologists think that Tyrian purple created a need for white wool that could be easily dyed. The first domestic sheep, like wild sheep, probably had grayish-brown coats. Shepherds in Middle Eastern countries began to mate sheep with light-colored coats, knowing that many of their offspring would also be light colored. By 1000 B.C., continuous breeding of light-colored sheep had led to sheep with white wool that took the purple dye well. This same breeding technology also led to sheep with pure black or gray wool that required no dyeing.

DOMESTICATING WHEAT

How did ancient people learn to domesticate plants such as wheat? The process was a little different from the domestication of animals. Hunter-gatherers in the Middle East probably lingered longer and longer near the immense fields of wild wheat that grew as the last ice age ended. At first, people probably only collected the wild grain to eat it. But they must have noticed that the grain could sprout into new plants.

Perhaps stored grain got wet, and ancient people saw it grow into seedlings. Maybe someone dropped a container of wild wheat seeds and noticed that a dense wheat patch grew in the same spot the next season. Maybe people made offerings to spirits by throwing seeds on the ground.

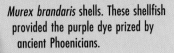

Murex brandaris shells. These shellfish provided the purple dye prized by ancient Phoenicians.

Technology's Other Side

Technology sometimes has two faces—one beneficial, one negative. Modern people are familiar with technology's unpleasant side. For instance, modern industry often pollutes the environment. The spread of modern agriculture sometimes destroys tropical rain forests and threatens plants and animals with extinction.

Technology was two-faced in ancient times, too. For instance, wherever Phoenicia established colonies in the Mediterranean region, colonists collected the shellfish *Murex brandaris* to make dye. Each shellfish yielded only a tiny amount of dye. People had to kill hundreds of thousands of shellfish to make just one gram (0.035 ounce) of dye. Huge mounds of shells mark the sites of ancient Phoenician colonies.

Archaeologists believe that dye production led to the extinction of two species of shellfish. Perhaps for the first time, technology had showed its negative face.

Then they realized that a great deal of wheat grew where the seeds had been scattered. In time, people began to scatter seeds intentionally.

There are two kinds of wild wheat, emmer and einkorn. Ancient people in the Middle East gathered both. Although these grains are good to eat, they have a frustrating trait. The ears of wild wheat shatter as the grain ripens. Wheat kernels break away from the ears and fall to the ground.

This trait is beneficial for wheat plants. It is nature's planting mechanism, assuring that seeds scatter over the soil. But imagine how frustrating it must have been for hunter-gatherers. They might find a dense stand of wild wheat, enough to feed many people, only to have the grains fall away when touched, or at the first stroke of stone knives.

Hunter-gatherers must have loved to find mutant wheat plants whose ears did not shatter. These plants were rare. Experts estimate that only one wild plant in every four million was a nonshattering mutant. People naturally harvested the rare, nonshattering ears and used them for seed. Gradually, the nonshattering mutant was domesticated and became the main wheat plant in the ancient Middle East. It could be harvested easily.

THE PLOW

Plows are devices that cut into the soil, preparing it for planting. We do not know exactly when or where the first plows were made. But archaeologists believe that plows were invented in the Middle East, soon after the start of agriculture there.

The first plows were probably made from forked tree

branches. A farmer would sharpen a branch and harden it in a fire. He then used the forked end of the branch as a handle and pushed or pulled the sharp point through the soil. (Farmers in some poor countries still use this kind of primitive plow.) People then realized that plows worked more efficiently if one person steered the plow while one or more persons pulled it with ropes.

Plows revolutionized agriculture. They saved great amounts of time and labor, allowing farmers to plant larger fields and grow more food. But the real revolution from plows came only when they were teamed up with another form of ancient technology—large draft animals.

Sheep and goats are too small and weak to pull plows through heavy soil. The only draft animals (*draft* means "pull") in the ancient Middle East were bulls, or male cattle. But bulls were too wild and violent to be harnessed to plows. Ancient farmers somehow realized that wild bulls could be converted into tame, manageable animals by castration—removing the testicles. A castrated bull is called an ox.

A wall painting made around 6500 B.C. at Çatalhüyük in the modern country of Turkey is the first known picture of an ox. It shows a bull obviously lacking its testicles. Archaeologists aren't sure whether this ox was used in agriculture or in religious ceremonies. The oldest surviving pictures of oxen hitched to plows were made around 3000 B.C. in Egypt and Mesopotamia.

Plows pulled by oxen allowed one farmer to cultivate more land in a single day than several farmers with hoes or spades could till in a week. Plows also allowed farmers to cultivate land that was packed too hard to be tilled with hand tools.

Later, plows were improved by adding iron blades and moldboards, curved plates that lifted and turned the soil. By 760 B.C., farmers in Assyria were using a combination plow-planter. This device consisted of a funnel attached to a wooden plow. Seeds poured into the funnel fell evenly into the furrows, or rows, created by the plow.

MOVING WATER

Irrigation, supplying crops with water, was hard work for ancient farmers. A gallon of water weighs about eight pounds. Plants in a typical field might require thousands of gallons of water each day. Early farmers used pottery jars and other containers to carry water from wells and rivers to their fields.

In about 2000 B.C., people in Mesopotamia and Egypt began using a device called a *shaduf* to make the work of irrigation easier. A shaduf is a long pole with a bucket on one end, a fulcrum (pivot point) in the center, and a weight on the other end. Shadufs allowed people to lift weight by using leverage rather than just brute force. By raising and lowering the weight on one end of a shaduf, a farmer could easily lift a bucket of water on the other end. People sometimes still use shadufs in places where there are no mechanical pumps.

ANCIENT KITCHENS

A big part of agricultural technology occurred not in fields but in kitchens. People had to develop ways of preparing, processing, and preserving the many new foods that agriculture introduced into the human diet.

Excavations in modern-day Iraq show that Middle Eastern

Assyrian stone carving of a shaduf, or water-sweep

people used kitchens 7,500 years ago. Archaeologists have found basic cooking equipment such as pots, jugs, and ladles in the remains of ancient farming villages. Ancient cooks also used flat bowls and trays for grinding grain and removing the inedible husks.

Ovens in the ancient Middle East were large clay domes that had been hardened by fire. Several families shared one large oven. A wood fire heated the oven, and bakers placed flat loaves of bread against the oven walls for baking. Sometimes, bakers placed loaves in the bottom of the oven, on hot rocks, with a few rocks placed on top of the loaves to speed baking. People in some Middle Eastern countries still bake flat loaves of bread in this way.

THE FIRST COOKBOOK

Agricultural technology also includes cooking. The world's oldest known recipes were written on clay tablets in ancient Babylon around 1700 B.C. Ancient recipes usually didn't give amounts of ingredients or cooking times. Cooks used their own judgment. But modern scholars say that ancient recipes would have made tasty and healthful dishes that included meat, vegetables, and starches.

Here are a few ancient Babylonian recipes translated by archaeologists at Yale University. Similar ingredients can be substituted for the ancient ingredients in these dishes. For example, chicken can be substituted for pigeon.

> **Bouillon of pigeon.** Open the pigeon in two. You also need some other meat. Place in water. Add fat, salt as you wish, cereal cake crumbled, onion and samidu [similar to an onion], leek and garlic and herbs earlier steeped in milk. Serve.

> **Lamb bouillon.** You need other meat too. Place in water. Add fat, salt as you wish, crumbled cereal cake, onion and samidu, coriander, cumin, leek, and garlic. Serve.

> **Bouillon with dodder** [an herb]. No need for fresh meat, but salted. Place in water. Add dodder in sufficient quantity; some onion and samidu; coriander and cumin; leek and garlic. Serve.

FERMENTATION

Fermentation is an important process, developed in ancient times and still used to prepare and preserve foods. During fermentation, foods undergo gradual chemical changes. Fermentation changes grape juice into wine, for instance, mashed grain into beer, and milk into cheese and yogurt.

Fermentation is also used in making bread, vinegar, and soy sauce.

Ancient people in the Middle East used fermentation to preserve food. For example, fresh milk sours and becomes undrinkable in a few days. But milk fermented into yogurt or cheese lasts much longer. Ancient people also used fermentation to make wine and other alcoholic drinks.

THE OLDEST WINE

One day in 1995, archaeologists at the University of Pennsylvania Museum in Philadelphia were examining an ancient pottery jar. The jar had been discovered in the kitchen of a mud-brick dwelling at an ancient village in northern Iran. Inside the jar, the archaeologists noticed a strange yellowish smudge.

The archaeologists were curious. They did not say, "Well, it is only a stain. We'll wash it out." They wanted to know what material had left the smudge. Deposits inside ancient pottery often give important information about the foods that people ate thousands of years ago.

Chemical tests showed that the smudge came from wine produced between about 5400 B.C. and 5000 B.C. The discovery startled archaeologists, because it showed that ancient people had made wine two thousand years earlier than was previously believed.

The smudge also contained traces of what may be one of the earliest food additives. It was resin, a saplike material, from the terebinth tree. The wine makers probably added terebinth resin to kill bacteria that would otherwise have changed the wine into vinegar. They might also have used terebinth to hide sour flavors in the wine.

But it certainly is difficult to imagine anyone drinking wine with terebinth resin. Another name for the terebinth tree is the turpentine tree. Ancient wine with terebinth resin would have smelled and tasted a bit like the strong solvent used to remove paint stains.

POTTERY

The agricultural revolution created a critical need for pottery. Farming people needed vessels to hold water for drinking, cooking, and irrigation. They also needed pots to hold milk, wine, olive oil, and other foods.

Nearly every ancient civilization produced pottery. Hunter-gatherers in Japan made the world's first known pottery vessel about 12,000 years ago. This round-bottomed pot was found at an ancient site near Nasunahara, Japan.

People in Mesopotamia took the first step in automating, or mechanizing, pottery production with the development of the potter's wheel. This rotating wooden disk allowed craftspeople to rapidly shape lumps of clay into vessels. Potters used their feet to turn the wheel. They used their hands to shape the bottom and sides of the clay pots.

Ancient potters then hardened the vessels by firing them in hot ovens. They also learned to coat pots with certain minerals from the soil before firing them. When heated, the minerals formed a glaze, or waterproof coating.

The ancient people who made the first pottery probably didn't care how it looked, so long as it was sturdy. But potters gradually developed techniques for using different clays and different firing temperatures to make pottery that was red, brown, buff, or black. They painted designs on the surface of pots to create works of art.

Archaeologists sometimes date the advance of a civilization by noting different stages in its pottery-making technology. Some experts regard pottery making as the first pyrotechnology—the use of fire to make products.

THE FIRST FABRICS

Making plant and animal fibers into fabric, or cloth, is also a kind of agricultural technology. Ancient people made fabric sacks to hold food and other materials. But mostly they used fabric as clothing.

People in warm parts of the ancient Middle East usually wore simple, loose-fitting clothing that was well suited to a hot climate. The loincloth, a piece of fabric wrapped around the hips and fastened at the waist, was the basic garment for men.

Women often wore rectangular pieces of cloth, wrapped around the body and fastened at the shoulder and waist. The Persians and other groups who lived in cooler climates wore trousers, robes, and tunics.

Felt made from the wool of animals was an important fabric in the ancient Middle East. Felt was used to make clothing, especially heavy garments for cold weather. The ancient Persians made felt caps with earflaps. Such caps were similar in style to caps that are still worn in some parts of the world.

Felt is not woven like most other kinds of fabric. Instead, felt is made from compressed wool fibers, locked together into a dense tangle. Felt forms naturally in the coats of sheep that are molting, or shedding, their wool. Ancient shepherds may have gathered natural felt and used it as a model for felt making. One legend claims that felt was discovered when ancient people lined their boots with wool. The weight, heat, and moisture of people's feet compressed the wool into sheets of felt fabric.

LOOMS

Ancient people also made fabric by weaving wool, camel hair, flax, hemp, cotton, and other fibers on a device called a loom. During weaving, two sets of fibers are interlaced at right angles. You can see this pattern yourself by looking through a magnifying glass at the tiny threads in cotton cloth.

Ancient Chinese and Middle Eastern craftspeople made simple hand looms. These were small wooden frames that kept threads under tension while others were interlaced with them. Variations on this basic design were used until 1733, when a British inventor named John Kay introduced new technology that greatly increased the speed of weaving.

ANCIENT EGYPT

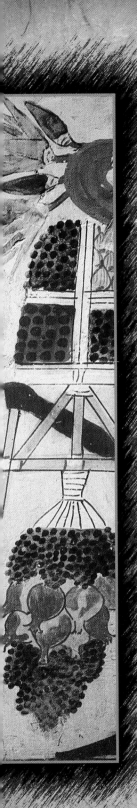

Depiction of harvest offerings, from the Tomb of Nakht

Civilization in Egypt grew because of agriculture along the Nile River. The Nile is the world's longest river. It flows north 4,145 miles from Lake Victoria in the mountains of modern Uganda and Tanzania to the Mediterranean Sea.

Ancient hunters and gatherers moved toward the Nile around 8000 B.C. as the climate in northern Africa became drier. By about 7000 B.C., people had built permanent settlements along the river. Probably one of the reasons people moved close to the Nile was that abundant fields of wild grain grew there.

Every summer, when rainwater that had fallen earlier in Uganda and Tanzania finally reached Egypt, the Nile flooded its banks. Floodwaters soaked the dry soil and left fertile, mudlike silt that was perfect for growing crops.

When the flooding ended in early autumn, Egyptian farmers had to work quickly to prepare fields for planting. If they waited too long,

41

the hot sun would quickly bake the wet soil into rock-hard clay. With domesticated animals, two-handled plows, and other farming technology introduced from the Middle East, Egypt became one of the greatest wheat producers in the ancient world.

Egyptian farmers also grew cotton; a grain called millet; and flax, which was woven into linen. They herded goats and sheep and raised pigs. They also kept some unusual animals—gazelles, deer, Barbary sheep, even hyenas—that are

Egyptian limestone fragment showing a monkey in a tree, made around 1350–1250 B.C.

no longer domesticated. Egyptian farmers even kept monkeys, who were trained to pick fruit from tree branches. A painting inside an Egyptian tomb from 1900 B.C. shows monkeys picking fruit from treetops and handing it to people on the ground.

BIG PROJECTS

Around 3100 B.C., a ruler named Menes united Egypt and established its first dynasty, or ruling family. One of King Menes' first great achievements after unifying Egypt was construction of an irrigation project.

Irrigation involves damming rivers, digging canals, and devising other systems for moving, lifting, and controlling water. Irrigated land yields about twice as much food per acre as nonirrigated land, so many ancient civilizations relied heavily on irrigation to increase food supplies.

Evidence suggests that the Egyptians irrigated land along the Nile beginning about 5000 B.C. The Sumerians began to use irrigation around 2400 B.C., and the Chinese began around 2200 B.C.

The Egyptians even established a "Department of Irrigation," a government agency, around 2800 B.C. One irrigation project was a dam on the Nile, built around 2500 B.C. to supply water to a stone quarry south of Cairo. The dam was almost 350 feet long, 40 feet high, and 78 feet thick at the base.

In another project, the Egyptians dug a 12-mile-long canal from the Nile to Lake Moeris. When the Nile flooded, water flowed through the canal to the lake, where it was stored for year-round use in irrigation.

The Egyptian government also had an agency to oversee agriculture. The United States has a department of agriculture, headed by a secretary of agriculture. In ancient Egypt, this job was held by the grand vizier. Only the pharaoh, Egypt's chief ruler, had more power. The grand vizier and his staff supervised irrigation, grain and livestock production, and relations between landlords and tenant farmers.

FIRST FISHING ROD?

The oldest known painting of a fishing rod comes from an Egyptian tomb built around 2000 B.C. The painting shows a nobleman sitting in an ornate chair in his garden and holding a fishing pole. The line drops into a rectangular pond filled with fish.

Archaeologists believe that some rich Egyptians, like the man in the painting, dug channels from the Nile River into their backyards so they could fish in comfort. Other Egyptian people fished from the banks of the Nile or from boats. Egyptians probably fished for both sport and a tasty meal.

BEER . . .

Bread and butter are staples, or basics, of the American diet. In ancient Egypt, bread and *beer* were staples. Both were made from emmer wheat. But Egyptians did not drink beer just to quench their thirst. Ancient Egyptian beer was thick, cloudy, and healthful. Beer was an important part of the diet in other ancient lands, as well.

When did people first brew beer? Archaeologists have found beer residue inside a jar used in Mesopotamia between 3500 and 3100 B.C. The ancient Mesopotamian symbol for beer was a group of horizontal, vertical, or crisscross lines. The clay jar with the beer residue was marked with that symbol.

Fresco depicting men fishing in a papyrus thicket, from the tomb of the sculptor Ipuis

... AND BREAD

Delwen Samuel couldn't wait to do two things with the loaves of bread baking in her oven one day in 1996. The bread smelled delicious, and Samuel wanted to taste it. But she also wanted to study it.

Samuel, an archaeologist at the University of Cambridge in England, had baked the bread to test her theories about Egyptian bread-making technology. Archaeologists long believed that ancient Egyptian bread was coarse and gritty, because it was made from emmer wheat, which has a tough outer hull that is difficult to remove.

Samuel had studied microscopic starch granules in fossilized loaves of bread, baked in Egypt around 2000 B.C. By studying the granules, Samuel figured out how Egyptians made emmer flour and emmer bread. She thinks the Egyptian bakers wet the emmer wheat, allowed it to sprout, dried it, ground it into flour, and used lots and lots of water in the dough.

How could Samuel test her conclusions? She baked bread using the same procedures. She reported that the slices were rich, sweet, and "rather tasty."

THE FIRST BEEKEEPERS

Ancient Egyptians used lots of honey—as food, medicine, and a gift to the gods. One scientist figured that Rameses III, who ruled Egypt from 1198 to 1166 B.C., set aside 15 tons of honey for the gods in one year. The Egyptians needed much more honey than they could get by robbing wild beehives.

So, around 2500 B.C., the Egyptians began raising their own bees. A stone carving on an Egyptian temple at Abu Ghorab depicts the beekeeping process. The carving shows beehives made from cylinders of dried mud. It shows people taking bees from the hives, removing honey, separating the wax, and storing honey in pottery jars.

ANCIENT CHINA

Mention food and China, and many people think of rice. Rice is indeed an important crop in China. But it was not the first grain domesticated there. About nine thousand years ago, farmers in northern China grew millet—which is still a major crop in China and other parts of the world. Ancient Chinese farmers also grew wheat, soybeans, barley, and other grains.

Rice cultivation in China began more than eight thousand years ago in the warm, moist Yangtze River valley. Wild rice grew throughout this area, and Chinese hunter-gatherers gradually learned to save and plant rice seeds. Because the soil was wet and heavy, rice farmers needed sturdy tools. They used strong spades, with wooden handles and blades made from the shoulder bones of buffaloes.

PUDDLING RICE

Rice is the modern world's number-one food crop and a staple food for about 2.4 billion

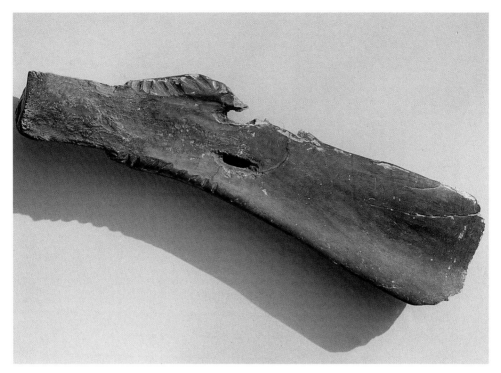

Buffalo-bone spade made around 4000 B.C. from Zhejiang, China

people. Rice became such an important food because of a farming technique perfected in ancient China.

The first Chinese farmers probably planted rice seeds directly into the soil, where they grew into mature plants. But weeds tended to spring up along with the rice plants. So fields needed constant weeding. Since rice plants need a lot of water, crops also suffered during dry weather.

Around 800 B.C., Chinese farmers discovered they could grow more rice if seedlings were transplanted into flooded fields, or paddies. The process was called puddling. In flooded fields, rice plants got plenty of water, even during dry spells. In addition, weeds couldn't grow in the flooded fields. Puddling and transplanting completed the domestication of rice. Most of the world's rice still is grown in this way.

AGRICULTURE AND SOCIETY

Technology can affect society in many ways. For instance, puddling not only improved the rice crop but also helped bind ancient Chinese society together. Here's why.

Growing rice in flooded fields required much more labor and care than growing crops on dry land. People had to work together. They had to build fields with a slight grade, or slope, to keep water moving from one paddy to the next. They had to build barriers to keep water in the fields. They had to watch for approaching rainstorms. They had to raise and lower control gates so that water would not be wasted. They had to build canals and reservoirs.

Puddling forced people to cooperate, organize, specialize in different kinds of work, and follow work schedules. People depended on one another to get the job done, so civilization in China became more structured.

BIOLOGICAL PEST CONTROL

Insects and other pests destroy about 35 percent of all crops worldwide. Biological pest control involves killing insects—not with poisonous chemicals but with the pests' own natural enemies. For instance, ladybugs, wasps, and even some microbes are natural "insecticides" that can kill pests without damaging crops. Biological pest control may seem like the latest high-tech weapon against insects. But biological pest control is not new. The ancient Chinese used the technology at least two thousand years ago.

For example, Chinese farmers released large insects called praying mantises into flower and vegetable fields. The mantises fed on smaller insects that could damage crops. In some regions of ancient China, it was illegal to kill frogs. Why? Because frogs ate huge amounts of insects that damaged crops. In another pest control method, Chinese fruit farmers hung burning torches in tree branches. Insects were attracted to the firelight and burned up when they approached.

Chinese farmers used other methods to keep rats, fungi, weeds, and other pests from damaging seeds, crops, and grain. Sometime around A.D. 100, the Chinese discovered that chrysanthemum flowers, dried and ground into a fine powder, killed insects on vegetable plants. The active ingredient in chrysanthemum is a chemical called pyrethrum. Many modern vegetable gardeners use pyrethrum to kill insects. It does not harm the environment and is not toxic to animals other than insects.

Consumers in ancient China paid high prices for mandarin oranges—small, lusciously sweet citrus fruits that people still enjoy. Like modern consumers, people in ancient China wanted flawless fruit for their money. Ancient Chinese fruit growers protected their oranges from harmful insects with the help of carnivorous ants called yellow citrus killer ants. To collect the ants, people placed leather bags filled with grease and straw next to ant mounds. Ants were attracted to the grease, so they entered the bags, which were then sold to orange growers. Growers released the ants into their fruit trees and sometimes even built little bamboo bridges from tree to tree to help ants spread throughout the groves. In a book called *Records of Plants and Trees of the Southern Regions,* Xi Han, a Chinese writer who lived in the A.D. 300s, described how killer ants were used:

> The bags are attached to twigs and leaves. The ants are reddish-yellow in color, bigger than ordinary ants. These ants do not eat the oranges, but attack and kill insects which do. In the south, if the mandarin orange trees do not have this kind of ant, the fruits will be damaged by many harmful insects, and not a single fruit will be perfect.

Many American farmers seek advice on pest control and other issues from agricultural agents—specially trained members of the U.S. Department of Agriculture. Some of the world's first agricultural agents were appointed by the ancient Chinese government around 300 B.C. The agents gave farmers advice on every stage of agriculture, from soil preparation before planting to storage and transportation of the harvest.

ANCIENT TECHNOLOGY REDISCOVERED

Modern scientists can learn a lot from the ancient Chinese. For instance, scientists are excited about a technology called mixed-stock rearing. In this process, farmers raise ducks, geese, rabbits, and other animals in and around fish ponds. The animals' droppings enrich the soil in the ponds and make good fertilizer for water plants. Fish eat the plants and grow to enormous size. After a few years of raising fish, farmers drain the fish ponds and grow grain in the fertile soil.

But the technique isn't new. The ancient Chinese pioneered mixed-stock rearing more than three thousand years ago. Chinese farmers raised carp (a kind of fish) in ponds and kept pigs along the shore. The pigs' droppings added fertilizer to the ponds. After raising carp for a time, farmers drained the ponds and used them as rice fields. Thus Chinese farmers got bountiful harvests from both the water and the land.

PEARL MAKERS

Raising fish, shrimp, clams, and other water animals is called aquaculture. Farmers mostly practice aquaculture to produce food. But one kind of aquaculture involves producing not food but valuable gems: pearls.

Pearls come from oysters. Oysters create pearls naturally when irritants enter their shells. To get more pearls, the ancient Chinese began putting sand and other material into oysters' shells. The material irritated the oysters, much as a cinder irritates a person's eye. But oysters don't secrete tears in response to the irritation. They secrete nacre, or mother-of-pearl, a lustrous material that coats the irritant. The layers and layers of coating make a pearl. The ancient Chinese were the first people to produce "cultured" pearls—pearls that were created deliberately rather than naturally.

DOMESTICATING A WORM

The Chinese domesticated many animals. In fact, they even domesticated a worm! Actually, it was the caterpillar of the silkworm moth, used to make silk.

Silk is one of the oldest textiles in the world and one of the most valuable. Merchants in ancient Rome had a simple way of setting the price of a piece of silk: they weighed the silk and traded it for an equal weight of gold! Chinese legends say that silk was made as long ago as 2700 B.C.

Silkworm moths come from China, and people there devised the complicated technique for turning the moths' cocoons into silk fiber and fabric. Tiny eggs of the silkworm moth had to be kept warm until the caterpillars hatched. The caterpillars were fed for six weeks on chopped mulberry leaves. Then they spun silken cocoons on branches.

Silkworms feeding on mulberry leaves

Silk fragments from A.D. 300–500, found at the Silk Road city of Dunhuang, China

Farmers boiled the cocoons to remove the sticky substance holding the silk in place. They unwound the silk from the cocoons, and twisted together silk from several cocoons to form thread. The silk thread could then be woven into fabric.

Each cocoon contained only a small amount of silk. About 2,700 silkworms gave just one pound of fabric. No wonder silk was so expensive.

There are no records of who invented the silk-making

process. The ancient Chinese kept the process a carefully guarded secret. Since no one else knew how to make silk, the entire world had to buy its silk from China.

In A.D. 300, people in Japan and India discovered the secret and began making and selling their own silk. In A.D. 550, the Roman emperor Justinian I sent two monks on a spying mission to China. The monks learned the secret, stole mulberry seeds and silkworm eggs, hid them inside their walking staffs, and brought them to the West.

ANCIENT ICE CREAM

Have you heard the story of how Marco Polo, an Italian traveler who lived from A.D. 1254 to 1324, "discovered" ice cream when visiting China? Marco Polo probably did eat ice cream in China. But experts believe the ancient Chinese made ice cream thousands of years before Marco Polo arrived there.

The Chinese made the first ice cream around 2000 B.C. by freezing a mixture of milk, cream, honey, and flavoring. They also invented the first ice-cream maker by placing a container of milk, cream, and other ingredients inside a larger container filled with ice, water, and a salty material. Salt mixed with ice produces very cold temperatures, so the ingredients in the smaller container quickly froze into ice cream. Modern ice-cream makers still use salt and ice.

TEA AND COFFEE

Tea and coffee must be very old drinks, indeed. Right?

Not really. The first evidence of tea drinking comes from southern China around 50 B.C. People soaked dried leaves of the tea plant in hot water and drank the warm liquid as a medicine. Gradually, the custom spread to other parts of China. People eventually began drinking tea for its stimulant effects. Like coffee, tea contains caffeine, a chemical that stimulates the nervous system.

Coffee is a more modern drink. The first records of its use come from a Persian physician, Rhazes, who wrote about the drink around A.D. 920, centuries after the end of ancient times.

chapter five

ANCIENT AMERICAS

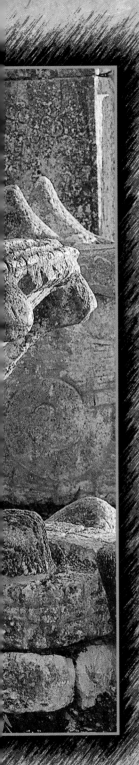

Statue of Kukulcán at the Temple of
Warriors, Yucatán, Mexico

Like early people in the Old World, the
first North Americans were hunters and
gatherers. They came to North America
from Siberia—following herds of bison,
mastodons, and mammoths—about 30,000
years ago. At that time, a land bridge called
Beringia linked Siberia and Alaska. Stone Age
people from Asia probably walked over this
bridge, or over thick ice in the Bering Strait.
Other people may have arrived in the New
World by boat over open stretches of ocean.

These Paleo-Indians (ancient Indians) then
moved south through Canada, into the American Great Plains, and into Mexico and Central
America. They reached the tip of South America
by about 9000 B.C. Different groups encountered different environments as they migrated
south, and separate cultures developed.

We have no written information about Paleo-
Indian food and agriculture and very few arti-
facts, or physical remains. But experts think

61

that the first Americans began to grow crops around 10,000 years ago. The evidence comes from a cave in Mexico, where scientists found domesticated squash seeds. When planted, the seeds grew into plants producing squash with thicker stems than wild squash have.

NEW FOODS

Gradually, great New World civilizations emerged, including the Olmecs, Maya, Toltecs, and Aztecs. These groups built big cities and empires in Mesoamerica (Mexico and Central America). They developed advanced farming techniques and were able to feed large populations. Some experts

Corn god statuette made by the Zapotec culture of southern Mexico

think that about 60 percent of the world's food—including corn, potatoes, and beans—was originally domesticated in the ancient Americas.

The ancient Maya grew maize (corn), squash, and beans. Farmers in Peru and Bolivia domesticated potatoes. Other New World foods included such modern-day favorites as chocolate, chili peppers, chewing gum, peanuts, pineapples, vanilla, tomatoes, and avocados. Unfortunately, the New World also gave us dangerous stimulants—tobacco and cocaine.

People in Europe knew nothing about corn, potatoes, tomatoes, chocolate, or other American crops until the fifteenth and sixteenth centuries, when Christopher Columbus and other explorers began bringing the plants back home. These crops quickly spread throughout the rest of the world and remain important sources of food.

CORN

Corn, or maize, is the world's third most important food crop—behind rice and wheat. Corn is the biggest grain crop in the United States. Sweet corn, often eaten on the cob, accounts for only a small part of the total corn production, however.

Most corn isn't eaten by people directly but is used in ways we often don't even realize. Corn gives us corn syrup, which is used to sweeten soft drinks, candy, baked goods, and other foods. Corn is fed to chickens, pigs, cows, and other livestock. People even use corn to produce an alcohol that makes gasoline burn cleaner (with less pollution).

Ancient people in Mesoamerica domesticated corn at least three thousand years ago. Corn was the basic food of ancient civilizations like the Maya. The crop then spread to the rest of the Americas—to Canada in the north and Argentina in the south.

BEANS WITH BAD VALVES

People in the Andes Mountains in Peru began growing beans at least eight thousand years ago. They picked a natural! Beans are healthful, grow well in poor soil, and can be dried and stored for use in cold winter months when other food is scarce. Modern farmers grow more than a hundred different kinds of beans, including navy, red, black, lima, and pinto beans.

But domestic beans had a wild ancestor with a frustrating trait. When a wild bean matures, the pod splits open and ejects the edible seeds. This "pod valve" is good for the bean. It is nature's way of spreading bean seeds and making sure they grow into new plants each season. The valve was bad for early farmers, however, since seeds often shot out of the pod before anyone could collect them.

Ancient farmers probably collected beans with "bad" valves—pods that didn't split easily or didn't split at all. Farmers saved these beans for planting. Many of the beans grew into plants with bad valves. Their seeds stayed in the pods until people came along for the harvest. It probably took a long time, but this practice of harvesting and planting beans with bad pod valves eventually gave modern society a favorite food.

CORN + BEANS = DIETARY DYNAMITE

When ancient people in the Americas ate corn and beans, they stumbled onto a nearly perfect food combination.

Both beans and corn are healthful foods. But neither contains the full variety of amino acids that the human body needs. Amino acids are essential to good health.

Corn is low in one amino acid, called lysine, and especially rich in another, called methionine. Beans are rich in lysine but low in methionine. Eaten together, beans and corn provide the body with its full assortment of amino acids. As an added benefit to farmers, both plants can grow together in the same field—along with another ancient American mainstay, squash.

SLASH AND BURN

The first farmers in Mesoamerica used a technique called slash-and-burn agriculture. Using stone axes, they chopped down trees in a section of forest. When the wood dried out, farmers set the field on fire. Burning cleared the land and left ash that was rich in nutrients for crops.

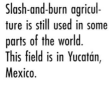

Slash-and-burn agriculture is still used in some parts of the world. This field is in Yucatán, Mexico.

Then farmers planted corn in the cleared fields, perhaps combined with beans and squash. After a few years of planting, the soil in the field lost its fertility, and the farmers moved on to slash, burn, and plant another area of forest.

ADVANCED TECHNOLOGY

The Maya developed an advanced system of agriculture. Their region of Mesoamerica has a wet season and a dry season. During the six-month wet season, rain often falls daily. Ancient farmers needed to save some of this water for use during the dry season. So they collected rainwater

Depiction of a farmer on a vase made by the Nazca culture of Peru

in ditches and other natural reservoirs. They built canals, irrigation channels, and small dams that helped them move water to and from reservoirs.

Mayan farmers also dug drainage ditches to dry out swampy soil. They rotated crops to preserve soil fertility. They mulched crops, covering the ground with layers of leaves to preserve moisture in the soil.

Another important technique involved raised fields—elevated plots of land piled up with fertile soil. The Maya sometimes built these fields between irrigation ditches. They dredged nutrient-rich muck from the bottom of the ditches and used it as fertilizer. The irrigation ditches also supplied plant roots with water.

Some archaeologists believe the Maya began using raised fields as early as 1000 B.C. As the Mayan empire expanded and its population grew, farmers needed to produce more food. Mayan agriculture reached its peak about A.D. 300, when the population was at its greatest.

CHEWING GUM

Sapodilla trees are big evergreens that grow wild in the rain forest. They produce a delicious brown fruit that tastes like a pear. They also produce a milky sap called chicle. Chicle can be boiled to remove water, then kneaded into a thick, tasteless, gummy substance. Add sweetener and flavoring, and you have chewing gum.

Who invented chewing gum? You may have read that an American photographer named Thomas Adams created gum in 1870 as a substitute for chewing tobacco. Actually, the ancient Maya collected and chewed chicle thousands of years earlier. We don't know if the Maya flavored their chicle.

The Maya worshipped many gods. One of the most important was Kukulcán, known to the Toltecs and Aztecs as Quetzalcoatl. Chicle was so important in Mesoamerican life that some pictures portray the god chewing a wad of gum.

When the modern world "discovered" chewing gum in the nineteenth century, the demand for chicle grew. People in Central America went deep into the rain forest to gather chicle from sapodilla trees. The popularity of gum led to a greater understanding of the ancient world. As people went farther into the forest to find chicle, they discovered many ruins of ancient Mesoamerican civilizations.

"FOOD OF THE GODS"

The cacao tree is a beautiful evergreen that grows wild in tropical areas. The tree's scientific name is *Theobroma cacao*. *Theobroma* means "food of the gods." Many people still think of chocolate as food fit for the gods.

Archaeologists know that the ancient Maya made a chocolate drink from cacao seeds before A.D. 100. When Spanish conquistadors arrived in Mexico in 1519, the Aztecs were growing domestic cacao trees. We don't know when the trees were first domesticated.

Cacao beans were so valuable that the ancient Maya actually used them as money. Only very wealthy people were able to afford chocolate. The drink was very different from modern-day hot chocolate. The Maya roasted and ground cacao beans and mixed them with cold corn mash, water, hot chili peppers, and spices. Spanish conquistadors combined ground cacao beans with sugar and cinnamon and introduced the modern chocolate that we like to eat.

GUINEA PIGS

Mention guinea pigs and most people think of pets or laboratory animals that scientists use in medical research. But these small rodents were (and still are) an important source of food for people in South America.

Archaeologists think that hunter-gatherers in ancient South America ate guinea pigs as far back as 12,000 years ago. While studying ancient settlements in Venezuela, Peru, Ecuador, and Argentina, archaeologists found a great number of guinea pig bones dating to around 2500 B.C. This was probably when South American farmers first domesticated guinea pigs.

Guinea pigs have some traits that make them easy to domesticate. They reproduce rapidly, eat household scraps, can be raised in pens, and have tasty meat. Guinea pigs are attracted to the warmth and garbage of human settlements. Ancient people probably discovered nests of guinea pigs in the corners of their huts and began breeding the animals.

LLAMAS AND ALPACAS

Ancient South Americans domesticated other animals as well. About nine thousand years ago, ancient people in the Andes Mountains hunted guanacos and vicuñas. Gradually, ancient people domesticated the guanaco. It became the modern llama, a long-eared animal, three to four feet high at the shoulder, with long, thick wool. Male llamas were used as beasts of burden, to carry packs. Females were raised for their meat and milk. Wool and skins from both males and females were used to make cloth and leather.

The vicuña was domesticated into the modern alpaca, which is smaller than the llama. Alpacas were raised mainly for their long wool, which is silkier and straighter than sheep's wool. Ancient people in South America herded and bred llamas and alpacas much as Old World people herded and bred goats and sheep. The llama and alpaca are still important agricultural animals in South America.

ANCIENT GREECE

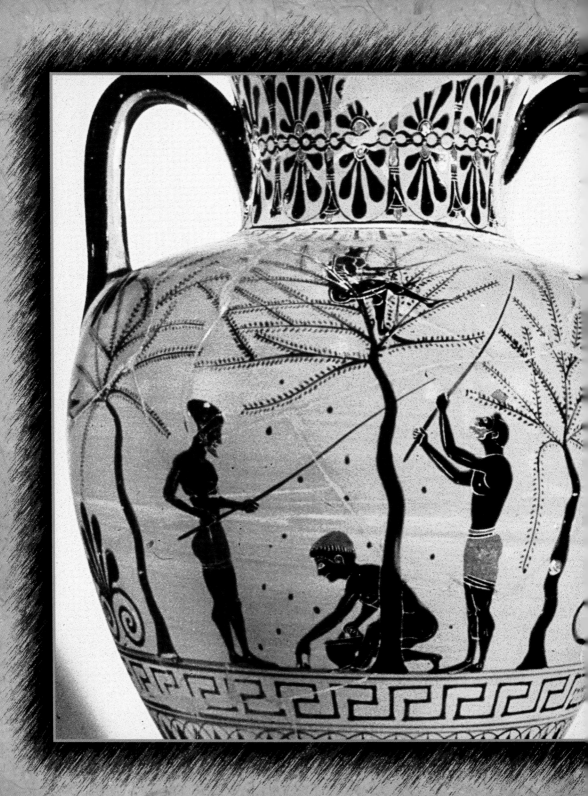

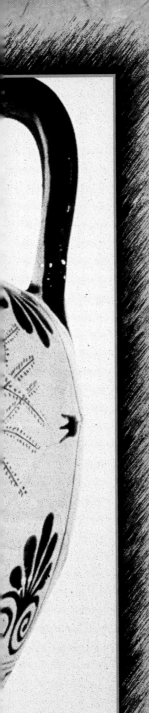

Olive harvesting shown on a Greek storage jar made around 520 B.C.

Strabo, an ancient Greek geographer and historian who lived from 63 B.C. to A.D. 24 once remarked, "The sea presses in upon the country with a thousand arms." Indeed Greece is mostly surrounded by water: the Aegean Sea to the east, the Ionian Sea to the west, and the Mediterranean Sea to the south. The ancient Greeks naturally looked to the surrounding ocean for food. They became great fishers. Fish and shellfish were an important part of their diet.

The ancient Greeks were also farmers. But Greece is a rugged, hilly land. Much of it is not well suited for farming, and ancient Greek farms were small. At first, Greek farmers harvested only wild olives and wild grapes to make oil and wine. In the 700s B.C., Greek farmers developed domestic olive trees that yielded more oil than wild trees. They grew improved kinds of grapes and other fruit.

LAERTES' FARM

What was the most famous farm in the ancient world? Many scholars pick a small farm that the Greek poet Homer described in *The Odyssey*. This great poem, written around 700 B.C., tells of the adventures of Odysseus as he tries to return home to Ithaca after the Trojan War.

Homer describes the farm owned by Odysseus's father, Laertes. "Everything is well cared for," Homer writes, "and there is never a plant, neither fig tree nor grapevine nor olive nor pear tree nor leek bed uncared for." Homer explains how Laertes fertilized plants with manure, irrigated his fields, and tried to boost yields in other ways. Laertes engaged in what modern farmers call intensive agriculture.

Laertes also used diversified agriculture. He raised a variety of crops that kept him and his workers busy all year. They reaped and threshed wheat and barley in early summer. They picked pears, figs, and other fruit in June, July, and August. In August and September, they harvested grapes and produced wine. Then came the planting of the next season's wheat. In between all these activities, the workers picked vegetables, ground grain into flour, and attended to many other chores. Some archaeologists believe that Laertes' farm was real, not just fictional, and they have searched for its ruins.

IRRIGATION SYSTEMS

Fruit trees and grapevines need a lot of water. They have to be irrigated for several years after planting, until they grow strong roots. Irrigation is especially important during the hot summer months.

Greece has no big river like the Nile to provide water

for large irrigation projects. So ancient Greek farmers built small irrigation systems. They dammed and diverted streams and springs and hoisted water from wells. In *The Odyssey*, Homer describes one farmer's irrigation system: a network of channels fed by two springs. Homer describes the results of the system:

> Fruit trees are grown tall and flourishing, pear and pomegranate trees and apple trees with their shiny fruit, and the sweet fig trees and the flourishing olive. Never is the fruit spoiled on these, never does it give out, neither in winter time nor summer, but always the West Wind blowing on the fruits brings some to ripeness while he starts others, pear matures on pear in that place, apple upon apple, grape cluster on grape cluster, fig on fig.

In another famous poem, *The Iliad*, Homer describes "a man running a channel from a spring of dark water who guides the run of the water among his plants and gardens with a mattock [a farm tool] in his hand and knocks down the blocks in the channel."

ARCHIMEDES' SCREW

For thousands of years, ancient farmers worked for many hours each day, hoisting buckets of water to irrigate their crops. The shaduf made this task easier. Ancient people eventually invented other machines that helped them move large amounts of water quickly. One device was a bucket chain—a series of buckets attached to a rope.

The great Greek engineer Archimedes of Syracuse developed a mechanical pump that made hoisting water even easier. He invented this pump, called Archimedes' screw, while studying in Alexandria, Egypt, the center of the scientific world in ancient times. The screw was used to pump water from the Nile River into wheat fields.

The screw was a hollow tube bent in the shape of a helix, which is a coil or spiral. The tube was wrapped around a shaft, with a cranklike handle on top. The bottom of the tube went into the water, and, with the device propped at about a 45-degree angle, workers turned the crank. As the crank rotated, water trapped in the loops of the spiral tube rose higher and higher until it spilled out at the top. Another version of the screw consisted of a spiral tube coiled inside a pipe.

Pumps based on this ancient design are easy to build, simple to operate, and very efficient. People in some developing countries still use Archimedes' screw to move water from one irrigation channel to another. Modern engineers also use screw pumps to move sewage in wastewater treatment plants.

MILLING GRAIN

One sound could be heard all day in most ancient households: the constant grate, grate, grate of people grinding grain by hand. Ancient people did this job with the help of stone mortars, pestles, and querns. A mortar was a small bowl for holding kernels of wheat or barley. A pestle was a rodlike tool for smashing grain inside a mortar. A quern was a flat stone that held kernels to be crushed with a roller. One person, working all day with these tools, could grind only enough flour to feed a few people. In a large household, several people had to work all day on the task.

But the sounds of grinding by hand began to disappear in ancient Greece around 100 B.C., with the start of

Mortar and pestle for grinding corn, found on the island of Cyprus

professional milling. Millers placed grain between big flat stones called millstones. Some stones were several feet wide. Big wooden spokes were attached to the stones, and slaves or animals turned the stones by walking in a circle.

The Greeks also used water power to grind grain. They laid a waterwheel flat in a stream. The current turned the wheel. Toothed gears attached to the wheel turned a shaft that turned millstones.

The Romans later introduced a more advanced mill. It had a movable, hourglass-shaped wooden pivot between the millstones. Adjusting the pivot changed the distance between the stones. So grain could be ground to different consistencies—fine for bread and coarse for porridge.

The Greeks were the master bakers of the ancient world. They made bread from different kinds of flour, including wheat, barley, and rye. Athenaeus, a Greek writer who lived around A.D. 200, compiled a list of more than 70 different kinds of bread made in Greece. Bakeries also sold cakes and pastries made from oat flour, honey, cream, dried fruits, and nuts. The Greeks even produced what may have been the world's first cheesecake.

ANCIENT EATING UTENSILS

The ancient Greeks are known as great philosophers, writers, and scholars. But they used the world's most unsophisticated eating utensils—their fingers. Their table manners were sloppy. They grabbed at plates of food, trying to gobble up the biggest and best pieces before anyone else.

The Greeks liked their meals served scalding hot, and they often burned their fingers while eating. One famous Greek gourmet, Philoxenus, trained himself to withstand the heat. He prepared his fingers by dipping them in hot water. He drank hot water, too, so he would be ready to gulp down the hottest morsels of food.

Some ancient people used more sophisticated eating utensils. Common people in China began using chopsticks between 400 and 300 B.C. Until then, only rich people used chopsticks. People in many ancient civilizations used knives and spoons as well as their fingers. But forks did not appear until the A.D. 500s, after the end of ancient times.

ANCIENT ROME

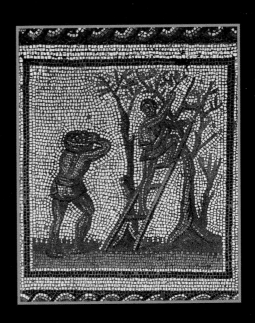

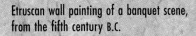

Etruscan wall painting of a banquet scene,
from the fifth century B.C.

A famous legend states that Romulus and Remus founded ancient Rome in 753 B.C. Romulus and Remus were twin sons of a princess from a nearby city. She left the infants to drown on the banks of the Tiber River, which was about to flood. According to the legend, a wolf found the boys and nursed and raised them. Romulus became the first king of Rome.

Actually, Roman civilization began long before Romulus and Remus. Historians believe that nomadic people called the Latins started grazing herds of sheep in central Italy around 2000 B.C. By 750 B.C., the Latins had settled into permanent farming villages. One village grew into the city of Rome.

The Romans were only one of many groups living in Italy. The Etruscans lived to the north and west. The Greeks had colonies in southern Italy and Sicily. In 509 B.C., the Romans overthrew the Etruscans, who had ruled them for a hundred years, and established a republic. The Roman republic lasted for five hundred years, and the Roman Empire lasted nearly another five hundred. During these years, Rome conquered many other countries and developed an empire that ruled much of the known world.

ROMAN FARMERS

Rome benefited from agricultural technology developed in conquered countries. Roman farmers used and improved on tools, seeds, seedlings, and techniques created earlier throughout the Mediterranean world.

The Romans also introduced new agricultural technology of their own. They left part of every field fallow, or unplanted, each year. In fallow soil, nutrients and water build up, and the soil becomes more fertile for the next season's planting.

The Romans also rotated, or alternated, the crops grown in a field. One year they would plant wheat, which robbed the soil of nitrogen, an important nutrient for crops. The next year they would plant legumes, such as beans, which replaced nitrogen and enriched the soil. Modern crop rotation methods are based on the ancient Roman practice.

ANCIENT TECHNOLOGY REDISCOVERED

Until the mid-1800s, farmers reaped grain by hand, cutting the stalks with big blades called scythes. It was slow, hard work. Then, in 1843, an Australian farmer named John Ridley developed a better way of reaping grain.

Ridley built a reaping machine made of a boxlike cart with one end open. A row of sharp metal blades—almost like the teeth on a comb—projected from the open end.

When the cart was pushed through a field, the blades caught on heads of grain and cut them from the stalks. The grain fell onto the cart. The reaper saved a lot of labor.

Guess where Ridley got the idea for the machine? Years earlier, he had seen a drawing of an ancient Roman reaper, used in France (which was then part of the Roman Empire) around A.D. 77. Ridley modeled his reaper after the Roman machine, called a *vallus*. The vallus was pushed by a donkey, with a man walking along to steer and add his strength. Ancient Romans also built a much larger reaper, called a *carpentum*, which was pushed by oxen.

But the Romans never took much advantage of the vallus, the carpentum, iron-bladed plows, or other farm technology. These devices were used on only a few farms in parts of the Roman Empire.

Coin from A.D. 90 showing a carpentum drawn by mules

WHY *NOT* THE REAPER?

Egypt was the ancient world's great wheat producer, and it supplied much of the grain Rome needed. In A.D. 16, the Romans imported about 16 million bushels of grain from Egypt and other North African countries just to feed the city of Rome. Instead of grain, Roman farmers focused on growing olives, grapes, and other fruits and vegetables.

But when sea winds were unfavorable and merchant ships could not reach Rome with grain shipments, the Roman people suffered shortages. They relied on the imported grain. They could not produce enough food to feed themselves.

Why did the Romans ignore technology such as the vallus and carpentum that would have helped them produce their own grain? Some experts think that Rome ignored the machines because grain from Africa was so cheap. Roman farmers could not compete with the low prices charged for imported grain. So they were not motivated to adopt better agricultural technology.

FISH FARMING

The Romans did take the lead in aquaculture, however. Though many ancient civilizations, including the Egyptians, Chinese, and Japanese, practiced aquaculture, some of the biggest and most elaborate fish farms were built in ancient Rome. Roman farmers bred freshwater fish in ponds and experimented with raising saltwater fish in freshwater lakes.

One big commercial fish farm was located at Cosa, a port north of Rome. The farm produced about three million pounds of fish each year. Its concrete tanks, supplied with seawater through a lagoon, covered 2.5 acres of land.

Roman fish farmers wanted to raise bigger, tastier, and faster-growing fish and shellfish. One Roman oyster farm, built around 100 B.C., used heated water to make oysters grow more quickly. The Romans bred only the largest fish, knowing that many of the offspring of large fish would also be large. They made sure that tanks weren't overcrowded. They even fed fish high-calorie diets enriched with olive oil and wine!

Some Romans liked to keep fish as pets. Many wealthy Romans had *piscinari*, big fish tanks that looked much like modern swimming pools. Antonia Augusta, mother of the emperor Claudius, even put expensive gold earrings on the head of her favorite lamprey (a fish similar to an eel).

GORGING

Most ordinary Romans lived on a simple diet of bread, olives, mashed beans, chickpeas, wine, cheese, salted fish, and small amounts of meat. For a special treat Romans ate wheat cakes dipped in honey or milk, or porridge made from bread crumbs and onions fried in olive oil.

But rich Romans feasted at lavish banquets. One writer described the banquets that Queen Cleopatra of Egypt gave for the Roman leader Marc Antony:

We have five or six courses of fish, oysters, mussels, sea hogs with asparagus. Then we have capons, pies, and patties of fish and venison, many kinds of sea fruits and lobsters and polypuses cooked in spicy sauces, and partridges, cutlets of deer and gazelles, pheasants inside sweet crusts, big game, piglets stuffed with becassins and quails, ducks and turkeys and peacocks roasted and served with all their wonderful feathers, woodcocks in all kinds of sauces, tunny fish.

Gazelle, fowl, fruits, and vegetables for a Roman banquet. The painting dates to approximately the second to fourth centuries A.D.

Wealthy Romans sometimes abused this abundance of food. They feasted until they were stuffed. Then, to eat and drink still more, they visited a small room just off the banquet chamber. The Romans called this room a *vomitorium*. There they stuck straws down their throats, vomited, and returned to the banquet.

SPICE LOVERS

People have used spices for thousands of years. Spices not only improve the flavor of foods, but they also help preserve it. Ancient people probably also used spices to hide the taste of spoiled food. By 2000 B.C., Middle Eastern merchants were trading cinnamon, pepper, and other Indian spices throughout the Mediterranean world—where spices were among the most valuable of products.

The ancient craving for spices reached a peak in the Roman Empire. An entire section of Rome, the Spice Quarter, was devoted to the processing and selling of cloves, ginger, camphor, nutmeg, black and white pepper, cinnamon, sandalwood, turmeric, frankincense, myrrh, balsam, and other spices. The Romans paid high prices in gold or silver for these spices, which were imported from the Far East—more than five thousand miles away. The Roman senate often debated about whether the heavy use of spices would bankrupt the empire!

ICE CUBES

The Romans also loved iced desserts. Nero, a Roman emperor who lived from A.D. 37 to 68, made the first known recipe for sorbet. The dessert was made of crushed fruit sweetened with honey and frozen in a device much like the ancient Chinese ice-cream maker. Ice was expensive, since it had to be transported great distances from mountaintops to cities. So desserts like sorbet were expensive.

The Romans loved iced drinks, too. They cooled wine and fruit juices before drinking them and put chips of ice and scoops of snow into their glasses to keep drinks chilled. Archaeologists have found drink coolers in Greek settlements dating to the sixth century B.C. The coolers consisted of two separate pottery jars, one inside the other. Wine went into the central jar, and ice or snow went into the outer one.

The Salt of the Earth

Humans and other animals need to eat small quantities of sodium chloride, or salt, each day for good health. Modern people tend to eat too much salt, especially in prepared foods and snacks. Too much salt sometimes leads to high blood pressure.

Thousands of years ago, humans devoted great time and effort to getting enough salt. People not only craved salty foods but also used salt to preserve and process foods. Salt kept fish and meat from spoiling. It was used to make cheese, pickled goods, and other foods. Farmers fed salt to their livestock. Salt also was important in the religious ceremonies of the ancient Greeks, Romans, Hebrews, and Christians.

How important was salt to ancient people? Can you think of any other food that has whole cities named in its honor? Some place names, such as Salzburg and Hallstatt in Austria, Halle in Belgium, and Halluin in France, are derived from Latin (*sal*) or Greek (*hals*) words for salt. The Anglo-Saxon term *wich* originally meant "a place where there is salt." That's how places such as Sandwich and Norwich in England got their names. Towns with natural salt deposits were important in the ancient world. They were centers for the salt trade and for the preservation of food by salting.

Some ancient towns were located on trading routes called "salt roads."

Modern-day salt production in Ethiopia

Caravans of camels, donkeys, and mules carried blocks of salt along these roads to market. One road extended from salt deposits in modern-day Ethiopia to markets in Egypt and Rome. Merchants sold salt in blocks, lumps, cakes, and sheets.

Can you think of any food so important that it was used as money? Salt was one of the first products that ancient people traded and one of the first forms of currency. Our word *salary* comes from the ancient Roman practice—the *salarium*—of paying soldiers partly in salt. If a man is not doing his job properly, we may describe him as "not worth his salt." We may praise another person by calling him or her "the salt of the earth."

People even fought over salt. Some ancient rulers placed heavy taxes on salt, and the taxpayers sometimes revolted. Ancient merchants battled pirates who tried to raid salt caravans and ships. As late as the sixteenth century, the countries of Mali and Morocco went to war over ownership of salt mines.

Salt was so important because of its essential role in the human diet and in food production. Butter or animal fat could replace olive oil. Sweet fruits could replace honey. Beans could replace meat. But there was no substitute for salt.

Ancient physicians and philosophers worried that iced drinks would cause stomach illnesses or turn people into weaklings. Lucius Seneca, a philosopher who lived from 4 B.C. to A.D. 65, complained about "skinny youths wrapped in cloaks and mufflers, pale and sickly, not only sipping snow but actually eating it and tossing bits into their glasses lest they become warm merely through the time taken in drinking."

ICE HOUSES

The Greeks and Romans used tremendous amounts of ice and snow, not just to cool drinks, but also for cold baths in summer, to preserve fish, and to keep other food from spoiling. Ancient Indians and Chinese also used ice to preserve meat, fruits, and vegetables.

Where did ancient people get snow and ice? They imported it on mule caravans from snow-covered mountain peaks. When caravans reached a city, merchants sold some of the supply to snow and ice shops that lined marketplaces. The rest went into storage in ice houses.

The ice houses were underground pits, sometimes more than 30 feet deep. The cool underground temperatures helped keep the ice from melting. A layer of straw, grass, or leaves sealed the pit opening and served as insulation, keeping cool air in the pit and warm air out.

Archaeologists believe that the Romans and Greeks learned how to build ice houses from people in the Middle East. A text from present-day Iraq, written around 1700 B.C., mentions the first known ice storage pit. The ancient Chinese also stored ice in deep underground pits.

HUNGRY?

The next time you munch on a snack or sit down to a meal, remember the ancient roots of modern foods. Think about all the foods and food preparation techniques that were developed in ancient times. Think about plows, ovens, mills, and other ancient tools that we still use to grow and prepare food.

And remember, without the contributions of ancient farmers, you might be a hunter-gatherer. Instead of grabbing food from the refrigerator or the microwave oven, you might be out searching for your next meal with a spear or a fishing pole!

GLOSSARY

agriculture—the science or occupation of growing crops and raising animals

aquaculture—raising fish, shellfish, or edible sea plants in an artificial environment

archaeologist—a scientist who studies people and societies of ancient times

biological pest control—techniques to control insects and weeds using the pests' natural enemies

cultivate—to prepare farmland and grow crops

domesticate—to tame; to change wild animals and plants into varieties better suited for human use

excavate—to dig into the earth to search for ancient remains

fermentation—a chemical change in a substance that is caused by living organisms such as yeast or bacteria. Fermentation is used to make wine, beer, cheese, bread, and other foods.

fossils—remains or traces of ancient plants and animals preserved in the earth's crust

hunter-gatherers—people who get food by hunting, fishing, and foraging rather than by growing it

irrigation—artificial systems of supplying crops with water

mutant—a new form of animal or plant resulting from genetic change

nutrients—substances in food or soil, such as vitamins or minerals, that provide nourishment to animals or plants

puddling—flooding fields; a process used in China to grow rice

slash-and-burn agriculture—chopping down and burning trees on a plot of ground, then planting crops in the cleared land

technology—knowledge applied to satisfy humans' needs and to make life easier, happier, and longer. Technology might consist of instruments, tools, and equipment or of ideas and procedures.

BIBLIOGRAPHY

Cohen, Mark Nathan. *The Food Crisis in Prehistory.* New Haven, Conn.: Yale University Press, 1977.

de Camp, L. Sprague. *The Ancient Engineers.* New York: Ballantine Books, 1988.

Hanson, Victor Davis. *The Other Greeks: The Family Farm and the Agrarian Roots of Western Civilization.* New York: The Free Press, 1995.

James, Peter, and Nick Thorpe. *Ancient Inventions.* New York: Ballantine Books, 1994.

Leonard, Jonathan N. *The First Farmers.* New York: Time-Life Books, 1973.

Ryder, Michael L. "The Evolution of the Fleece." *Scientific American* (January 1987): 112–19.

Salzberg, Hugh W. *From Caveman to Chemist.* Washington, D.C.: American Chemical Society Press, 1991.

Smith, Bruce D. *The Emergence of Agriculture.* New York: Scientific American Library, 1995.

Toussaint-Samat, Maguelonne. *A History of Food.* Cambridge, Mass.: Blackwell Reference, 1993.

Visser, Margaret. *Much Depends on Dinner.* New York: Grove Press, 1986.

INDEX

guinea pigs, 69

honey, 19, 46

ice, 87, 90
ice cream, 57
insect control, 51–53
irrigation methods: in Egypt, 43–44; in Greece, 74–75; in Mesoamerica, 66–67; in the Middle East, 32

Maya, 63–64, 66–68
Mesopotamia, 25, 31–32, 36
Mexico, 61–62, 65–66
Middle East, 24–38: domestication of goats and sheep, 26–27; domestication of wheat, 28, 30; fabrics, 37–38; fermentation, 34–35; irrigation methods, 32; kitchens, 32–34; looms, 38; plows, 30–32; pottery, 36–37; Tyrian purple dye, 27–29; wine, 35–36
mixed-stock rearing, 53–54

nutrition: corn and beans, complementary nature of, 64–65; Stone Age diet, 18–19

ovens, 33
oxen, 31

Paleo-Indians, 61
pearls, 54

Peru, 63–64
Phoenicians, 26–29
plow, 30–32
pottery, 36–37, 87

rice. *See* grain
Rome, 79–91: farming, 82–85; fish farming, 84–85; gorging, 85–86; ice, 87, 90; reaping grain, 82–84; spices, 86–87

salt, 88–89
sapodilla trees, 67–68
silk, 54–57
slash-and-burn agriculture, 65–66
South America, 61, 64, 69–70
spices, 86–87
Stone Age, 11–22: fishing, 14–16; food preservation, 16–17; underwater caching, 17–18
Sumerians, 25, 43

tea, 57–58
technology, negative aspects of, 29

wheat. *See* grain

Note: There are alternate spellings for some of the names mentioned in this book. Here are three examples:
Tyre or Sūr or Sour (Middle East)
Rameses or Ramses (Egypt)
Hsi Han or Xi Han (China)

ABOUT THE AUTHORS

Michael Woods is an award-winning science and medical writer with the Washington bureau of the *Toledo Blade* and the *Pittsburgh Post Gazette*. His articles and weekly health column, "The Medical Journal," appear in newspapers around the United States. Born in Dunkirk, New York, Mr. Woods developed a love for science and writing in childhood and studied both topics in school. His many awards include an honorary doctorate degree for helping to develop the profession of science writing. His previous work includes a children's book on Antarctica, where he has traveled on three expeditions.

Mary B. Woods is an elementary school librarian in the Fairfax County, Virginia, public school system. Born in New Rochelle, New York, Mrs. Woods studied history in college and later received a master's degree in library science. She is coauthor of a children's book on new discoveries about the ancient Maya civilization.

Photo Acknowledgments: The photographs in this book are reproduced courtesy of: Art Resource, NY: (Scala) p. 1, (Giraudon) pp. 66, 79; Ancient Art & Architecture Collection, Ltd.: (© Ronald Sheridan) pp. 2–3, 23, 24–25, 40–41, 56, 83, 86, (© Mary Jelliffe) p. 11, (© G. Tortoli) p. 62; Bridgeman Art Library, London/New York: (Vitlycke Museum, Tanum, Bohuslan, Sweden/Roget-Viollet, Paris) pp. 12–13, (Oxford University Museum of Natural History, UK) p. 16, (Bridgeman Art Library) p. 29, (Fitzwilliam Museum, University of Cambridge, UK) p. 42, (Mogao Caves, Dunhuang, Gansu Province, NW China) pp. 48–49, (British Museum, London, UK) p. 59; CM Dixon, pp. 21, 27, 71, 77; The Granger Collection, pp. 33, 39, 72–73; AKG London, pp. 45, 80–81; ChinaStock: (© Ru Suichu) p. 47, (© Liu Liqun) p. 50, (© Dennis Cox) p. 55; © Chuck Place, pp. 60–61; © Kenneth Garrett, p. 65; American Lutheran Church. Used by permission of Augsburg Fortress, pp. 88–89.

Front cover: The Granger Collection (left), Erich Lessing/Art Resource, NY (upper right), London Museum/E.T. Archive (lower right).

JAMES JOYCE

and his world

JAMES JOYCE

and his world

BY CHESTER G. ANDERSON

CHARLES SCRIBNER'S SONS

NEW YORK

Printed in Great Britain
Library of Congress Catalog Card Number 77–83678
ISBN *0–684–15510–9*

Howth Head, Baily Lighthouse and Dublin Bay.

EARLY IN JUNE 1895, WHEN JAMES JOYCE was thirteen years old, he and his younger brother Stanislaus played truant from Belvedere College. They planned to walk to the Pigeon House, an electric power-station out on a breakwater in Dublin Bay, near the mouth of the Liffey River. They were tired of school and make-believe adventures; their home life was dull, their Jesuit masters dull and authoritarian. They wanted real adventures, and they thought they might encounter reality at the far-off Pigeon House.

It was a mild, sunny morning and they were very happy. They walked to the North Strand Bridge over the Royal Canal, then north-eastward along the North Strand Road. Turning right when they reached the Tolka River, they walked south-eastward on the Wharf Road and then south to the quays on the north side of the Liffey. They watched the tall ships and the spectacle of Dublin's commerce. Not much had happened and it was already noon.

They crossed the Liffey in a ferry-boat, disappointed that none of the Norwegian sailors unloading a ship on the opposite quay had green eyes. By the time they had wandered into Ringsend, still more than a mile from the Pigeon House, they were tired and the day had grown sultry. They spent their money on some biscuits and raspberry lemonade, and leaving Ringsend Road crossed a field and sat down on a sloping bank near the Dodder River. It was too late now, and they were too tired, to reach the Pigeon House.

A shabby old man approached. He had great gaps in his mouth between his yellow teeth. He talked to the boys about romantic novels and about little boys

The Pigeon House. 'By the smell of her kelp they made the pigeon house. Like fun they did!' (*Finnegans Wake*)

View from the North Strand Bridge over the Royal Canal. 'I was the first-comer to the bridge as I lived nearest.' ('An Encounter')

having sweethearts with nice soft hair and nice soft white hands. Then he went off into the field and did something that frightened the boys. Stanislaus called the man a 'queer old josser' and they planned to escape.

When the queer old josser returned, he talked about boys being whipped. As he used the word *whipping* over and over again, James Joyce looked into the bottle-green eyes that stared from under the twitching forehead. The boys did escape, but Joyce realized that in some ways he had more in common with the old josser than he had with Stanislaus and his other schoolmates.

Ten years later Joyce formed this childhood experience into the *Dubliners* story called 'An Encounter'. By then he had fled from the spiritually paralyzing 'reality' of Dublin to a self-imposed exile. But though he was to live out his life in foreign parts, 'exiled in upon his ego . . . writing the mystery of himself in furniture', most of the furniture was the Dublin of his childhood and youth. For he had realized that his ordinary Dublin life showed forth or 'epiphanized' reality itself, from which he would forge, in the words of Stephen's vow at the end of the *Portrait*, in the smithy of his soul the uncreated conscience of his race.

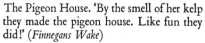

Barges of stout on the Liffey. 'We pleased ourselves with the spectacle of Dublin's commerce.' ▶
('An Encounter')

'We crossed the Liffey in the ferryboat, paying our toll to be transported in the company of two labourers.' ('An Encounter')

Pigeon House Road. 'It was too late and we were too tired to carry out our project of visiting the Pigeon House.' ('An Encounter')

As Joyce increased his distance from Dublin the temper of that conscience changed quickly from the aggressive sarcasm of his first fiction to the compassionate comedy of his last, where all of the enormities and frivolities of life and thought and history and art come gaily to the 'grand funferall' of *Finnegans Wake*. Even in 'An Encounter' the 'josser' is pidgin English for God, as the Pigeon House is Biblical and traditional English for the Holy Ghost: the sombre surface of the narrative veils the gay dance of a cosmic joke. But however joyous and liberating the comedy became, the serious quest for reality remained.

'Signatures of all things I am here to read, seaspawn and seawrack, the nearing tide, that rusty boot,' Stephen Dedalus thinks as he walks along Sandymount strand in *Ulysses*. Reader of signatures, Joyce came to understand his task as finding words to name what he read, so that others might read. The words he found were *Dubliners*, *A Portrait of the Artist as a Young Man*, *Ulysses*, and *Finnegans Wake*.

Joyce was born on 2 February 1882, at 41 Brighton Square (not a square but a triangle) in Rathgar, then a fashionable suburb on Dublin's south side. It was the first of a dozen brick houses which the Joyce family, increasing in size as rapidly as it declined in fortune, was to occupy during Joyce's early years.

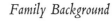

James was the first child of John Stanislaus and Mary Jane (May) Murray Joyce. Descended from the Norman-Irish Galway clan which gave its name to the Joyce Country, John came from Cork City, where he had loafed his extra-curricular way through Queen's College. His great-grandfather, George Joyce, had owned extensive properties in Cork, and at the time of his marriage

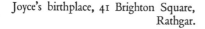

Joyce's birthplace, 41 Brighton Square, Rathgar.

May Murray Joyce. 'Her secrets: old feather fans, tasseled dancecards, powdered with musk, a gaud of amber beads in her locked drawer.' (*Ulysses*)

John Stanislaus Joyce, detail of a portrait by Patrick Tuohy. 'I was very fond of him always, being a sinner myself, and even liked his faults.' (*Letters*)

John Joyce still had the remains of his patrimony in addition to a sinecure in the office of the Collector-General of Rates and Taxes for the City of Dublin. Not yet bitter or mean, he was a good fellow, of infinite vitality and never at a loss. His drinking and spending were not yet thought excessive in a city of drinking spenders, and his quick wit and colourful language made him a character in the character-capital of the Western world.

Joyce's mother, ten years younger than John, was a gentle, pretty woman from Longford. Her father, John Murray, a wine merchant, had had business dealings with John Joyce when he was part-owner of a distilling company, a venture which failed. Murray opposed the marriage, and John Joyce repaid him with words: 'O weeping God, the things I married into.' His father-in-law, having married twice, became 'the old fornicator', his wife's brothers, William and John ('Red') Murray, both book-keepers, he called 'highly respectable gondoliers'.

These relatives received more enduring monuments in the work of John Joyce's son. May's brothers became Alphy and Joe in the story 'Clay'. 'Red' Murray appears under his own name in *Ulysses*. William appears as Richie Goulding in *Ulysses* and as the drunken Farrington in 'Counterparts'. It is Farrington's son who says, 'Don't beat me, pa! And I'll . . . I'll say a Hail Mary for you. . . .' – immortal words which Joyce took from the diary of his brother Stanislaus who recorded them from life. William's wife, Josephine, who remained Joyce's friend and confidante until her death, appears under her own name in the *Portrait*.

The Flynn side of May Murray's family was more acceptable to John Joyce. It was genteel and so musical that for fourteen years May was given piano and voice lessons. The Flynns and their house in Usher's Island (a quay, not an island, on the south bank of the Liffey) are well represented in 'The Dead', 'The Sisters' and elsewhere.

Ten children of the Joyce marriage survived infancy: James, born in 1882; Margaret ('Poppie') in 1884; Stanislaus in 1884; Charlie in 1886; George in 1887; Eileen in 1889; Mary (May) in 1890; Eva in 1891; Florence in 1892; and Mabel ('Baby') in 1893. Freddie, who died a few weeks after his birth in 1894, brought the number of live births up to eleven, one for each of the eleven mortgages which their progenitor placed on his Cork properties between late 1881, when James was in the womb, and 1894, when Freddie was born.

Joyce was formed in basic ways by his parents – less so by his brothers and sisters, who remained part of environment, a common heritage, and appear only fleetingly in his books. Stanislaus was the exception. Joyce maintained a close relationship with him throughout his life.

Joyce's Country, County Galway. ▶

His relationship with his 'nice mother', with her 'nicer smell than his father', was deeply emotional. She remained associated in his mind with warmth, home, fire and the Catholic faith. When he left the Church, her long-suffering faith accused him. He depended on her to quiz and praise his memory in childhood and to listen to his ideas and essays in youth. And dependent he remained in his image of sexual life – an image of 'surrender', of being 'held' and 'caressed', of assuming the inferior position.

If his attachment to his mother became guilt-ridden and emotionally umbilical, causing him to seek the extremes of prostitutes and 'blessed virgins', his detachment from his 'corked father' was comic. But his cool mockery should not hide Joyce's admiration of his father. He even took after him, not only as a spender and drinker and as a 'gentleman' proud of his ancestors, but also in his taste in music, his love of words and anecdote, his comic insight into the nature of things and his talent for mimicry.

It was probably from his father that Joyce got the habit of frequently moving house. In 1884 the Joyces moved from 41 Brighton Square to 23 Castlewood Avenue, and in May 1887 to 1 Martello Terrace, an attached house in Bray, and the first that Joyce used in his books. Bray, about ten miles south of Dublin, is a pretty sea-side village in the shadow of Bray Head.

The years at Bray were happy for the Joyce family. Living like a 'gracehoper', John joined the Bray Boat Club, rowed stroke in a four-man boat and entertained the club members informally. On at least one occasion his wife and eldest son appeared with him on the programme of a concert at the Boat Club. Week-end visitors used to come down by train from Dublin. Some of them

Martello Terrace, Bray (*left*); and the Esplanade and Bray Head. 'The Vances lived in number seven. They had a different father and mother.' (*A Portrait*)

James Joyce as a baby and at the age of two.

were political, like John Kelly of Tralee (John Casey in the *Portrait*), who rested at Bray between imprisonments for Land League agitation.

Most of the Joyce children were born by the time the family left Bray in 1892. The older ones played together, laying sieges by the sea-wall beside the house and putting on dramatic sketches in the front yard or the playroom on the third floor. Stanislaus's earliest memory of his older brother was of James playing Satan in an Adam and Eve skit.

The family was joined in Bray by John Joyce's uncle, William O'Connell from Cork (Uncle Charles in the *Portrait*) and by 'Dante' Hearn Conway, a bigoted Catholic and nationalist who taught Joyce reading, writing, arithmetic and geography. She is pictured in the *Portrait* as a 'spoiled nun' who kept a brush with a green velvet back for Parnell and another, with a red velvet back, for Michael Davitt, the founder of the Land League. From her Joyce learnt superstition and religious fear as well as the names of the mountains on the moon – then monuments to the work of Jesuit astronomers.

A chemist called James Vance and his family lived in one of the houses attached to the Joyces'. The Vances' eldest child, Eileen, only four months younger than Joyce, became his playmate, though Dante warned him that he would go to hell for playing with a Protestant. In the *Portrait* Joyce associates Eileen with the Blessed Virgin Mary:

> . . . when Dante was young . . . the protestants used to make fun of the litany of the Blessed Virgin. *Tower of Ivory*, they used to say, *House of Gold*. How could a woman be a tower of ivory or a house of gold?
>
> Eileen had long white hands. One evening when playing tig she put her hands over his eyes: long and white and thin and cold and soft. That was ivory: a cold white thing. That was the meaning of *Tower of Ivory*.

The passage illustrates the process – 'by thinking of things you could understand them' – which Joyce followed throughout his life. Looking intently at the world through words and at words through his experience of the world, he needed to name everything in his experience. His father once observed that if Joyce were dropped in the middle of the Sahara he would sit down and make a map of it.

Clongowes Wood College, County Kildare. 'A long shiver of fear flowed over his body. He saw the dark entrance hall of the castle.' (*A Portrait*)

On 1 September 1888, at the age of 'half-past-six', Joyce was taken by his parents to be enrolled in the finest Catholic preparatory school in Ireland, Clongowes Wood College, situated about twenty miles west of Dublin in the countryside near Clane. His mother kissed him and wept, and told him not to speak to the rough boys; his father gave him ten shillings, reminded him that his great-grandfather John O'Connell had given an address at Clongowes to the Liberator fifty years before, and told him never to peach on a fellow. Except for one brief spell, the Jesuits, who ran Clongowes, were to be Joyce's masters until he finished his university education in Dublin. He never recovered from their instruction. As Buck Mulligan in *Ulysses* says to Stephen, 'You have the cursed jesuit strain in you, only it's injected the wrong way.' In later life Joyce praised the Jesuits for teaching him 'to arrange things in such a way that they become easy to survey and to judge'.

Although the three years which Joyce spent at Clongowes were valuable to him and in general he was happy there, he was also home-sick. He

day-dreamed about going home for holidays and speculated about who he was and what his place was in the universe. The snobbish older boys tried to embarrass him about his father's social position and teased him about whether or not he kissed his mother before going to bed at night. While Clongowes seems to have had less of both homosexuality and sadism than the contemporary English schools described by George Orwell and Cyril Connolly, Joyce, as we learn from the *Portrait*, was introduced at Clongowes to 'smugging', a form of homosexual petting, and thought a good deal about the cruel hands of one of his masters and the feminine hands and manners of some schoolmates.

During his first months at the school the Prefect of Studies, Father James Daly ('Baldy-head' Dolan in the *Portrait* and *Ulysses*), beat his hands with a pandybat for breaking his glasses to avoid studying, though another boy had in fact broken them. The child Joyce, like the guiltless Stephen in the *Portrait* and like the adult Joyce of later years, appealed against this injustice to the highest authority available, the Reverend John Conmee, Rector of the College, and was vindicated when Father Conmee agreed to 'speak to Father Daly about it'.

This courageous act, combined with success in his studies, in which he led his class, earned Joyce the respect of his fellows and helped him to see himself as exceptional. He began to memorize long passages of verse and prose by Milton, Byron, Newman and others. This practice, which he continued throughout his life, coupled with the study of classical figures of rhetoric and the mastering of languages, led to the cultivation of his gift for mimetic style.

At Clongowes Joyce became devout; he received Communion regularly, wrote a hymn to the Blessed Virgin Mary and participated as boat-bearer in a procession to the little altar in the wood. His prayers and fantasies were filled with death and incantations against it. He was impressed – as he continued to be long after he had left the Church – by the dramatic form and the ceremonial costumes of the Church rituals.

At Clongowes he sang, took piano lessons, and is known to have acted in at least one play, taking the part of an imp. He played cricket and became a good swimmer, although his books suggest that he was a hydrophobe and disliked sports because of his poor physique and nearsightedness.

Joyce had a dread of physical violence that lasted throughout his life, and he was superstitiously afraid of thunderstorms, dogs and firearms. He was also obsessed by the idea of betrayal. In 1891, at the end of his second year at Clongowes, he was betrayed by a classmate – called Wells in both life and art – who shoved him into the cesspool ditch off the 'square' or 'yard', which was the boys' lavatory, because he refused to swop his little coffin-shaped snuff-box for Wells's seasoned hacking chestnut. As a result Joyce became ill with

IRISH LABOURER TO PARNELL:

"Whoever may forget you, I and mine shall always remember you gave us a home."

The popularity of Parnell after he had introduced a Tenants' Relief Bill in 1886.

the 'collywobbles' and never forgot the incident. Since there was no appeal, unless he were to 'peach on a fellow', he arraigned Wells in his books and secured his justice there.

Episodes like this intensified Joyce's longing for the holidays when he went home. The Christmas dinner scene in the *Portrait* is the best picture we have of one of these – the gay beginning as the shouting boys drive through the countryside to the Sallins railway station, the good fellowship at home as Simon Dedalus and Mr Casey discuss politics and the weather over their tinkling glasses of whisky, the disastrous change of tone as Dante objects to their proParnell and anticlerical talk in front of Stephen, and the hopelessness with which Mrs Dedalus and Uncle Charles try to make peace.

Parnell, charged with adultery before his death, was no longer acceptable to the bishops and priests of Ireland, not even to so nationalistic a soul as Dante. She had torn the green back off her Parnell brush. To Joyce, Parnell's morals mattered less than his aloofness, his mastery of politics; the Irish priests and people, as Joyce and his father saw it, had dragged their stag down like a pack of dogs. Joyce's first published work, no longer extant, was a poem about the betrayal entitled 'Et Tu, Healy', written in 1891 when he was nine; his proud father had it privately printed. That was the year – when, shortly before the Christmas dinner depicted in the *Portrait*, Parnell's body was returned to Ireland – in which Joyce began to see his own situation reflected in Parnell's and to model some of his mannerisms on those of the Chief. Like many other Irishmen, Joyce saw himself surrounded by enemies and friends, all scheming to do him wrong, and his suspicions, like those of other Irishmen, were often justified.

Shortly after Parnell's death, John Joyce's job in the Collector-General's office was abolished and he was pensioned off with £32 2s. 4d. a year. Only forty-two years old at the time, he never held a job again. His gradual descent into the world-renowned poverty of Dublin was cushioned by first the mortgaging and then the sale of his Cork properties, but the descent was inexorable.

An expression of anti-Parnell feelings after his marriage in June 1891.

A STARTLING CONTRAST.

THE WELL-MATCHED LEADER—" I and my *wife* are perfectly happy. As for myself, I may truly say that I am now enjoying greater happiness than I have experienced in the whole course of my previous life."
EVICTED TENANT—" What about me and my innocent *wife* and children, on whom the unbridled passions of you and that shameless woman have brought misery and ruin ?"

Joyce was withdrawn from Clongowes (his school bills partly unpaid) and the family moved to 23 Carysfort Avenue, Blackrock, another suburb on the coast, about half-way between Bray and Dublin. There Joyce studied by himself, wrote poems and part of a novel (now lost), and practised long-distance running under the tutelage of a crony of John Joyce's called Mike Flynn in the *Portrait*.

After about a year in Blackrock, the family moved into the north side of Dublin, to 14 Fitzgibbon Street, near Mountjoy Square. It was in this house that Joyce listened to his father's drunken monologue about his 'enemies'. For a time none of the children attended school, and Joyce wandered in the near-by streets, making 'a skeleton map of the city in his mind'. At first he went only as far as the neighbouring square and their parish church in Gardiner Street, the Jesuit Church of St Francis Xavier, but soon he walked all the way down Gardiner Street to the Custom House and the quays by the Liffey. During this interlude Joyce improved on the unsatisfactory reality in which he found himself by imagining an encounter with a real-life Mercedes (he had been reading *The Count of Monte Cristo*) during which he would be 'transfigured'. He saw himself, even more than he had earlier, as 'different from the others' – a child of destiny whose transfiguration would come 'without any overt act of his'.

The Joyces' home at 23 Carysfort Avenue, Blackrock.

The physical reality no doubt helped determine the kind of transfiguration that would come. Dublin is a city of patterns. Its neo-classical balance pervades the brick façades of its eighteenth-century buildings, the careful placing of its squares and greens, the harmonious arrangement of its streets, the situation of its public monuments, even the curves of its canals.

Nature itself supports the design: the city edges the middle portion of the bay, with Howth Head to the north and the Dalkey promontories to the south; the Liffey runs through the centre of the city, with the Dodder to the south, the Tolka to the north, and the Poddle in between, obligingly underground. Partly because of the patterns, partly because of the spaciousness which the patterns and waterways create, it is also a city of scenes and views. The dilapidation of these has, of course, been well known since Thackeray's time, certainly since Joyce's. But it must have made some difference to the development of Joyce's mind that it was the dilapidation of the age of reason.

For a few months the children were sent to the Christian Brothers' school ('with Paddy Stink and Micky Mud', as John Joyce contemptuously put it) a few blocks away in North Richmond Street. But in the spring of 1893, John Joyce managed to get James and Stanislaus admitted without fees to Belvedere College, a Jesuit day school in Great Denmark Street on the far side of Mountjoy Square.

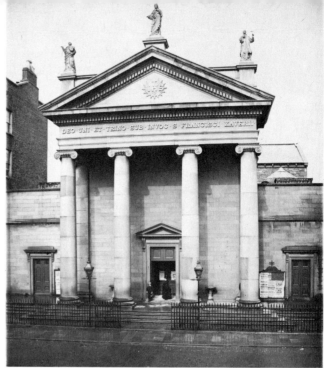

Young Joyce's Dublin:

a doorway in Mountjoy Square (*above left*),
the Church of St Francis Xavier (*above right*),
the chapel of Belvedere College (*below*),
the Custom House on the Liffey (*right*).

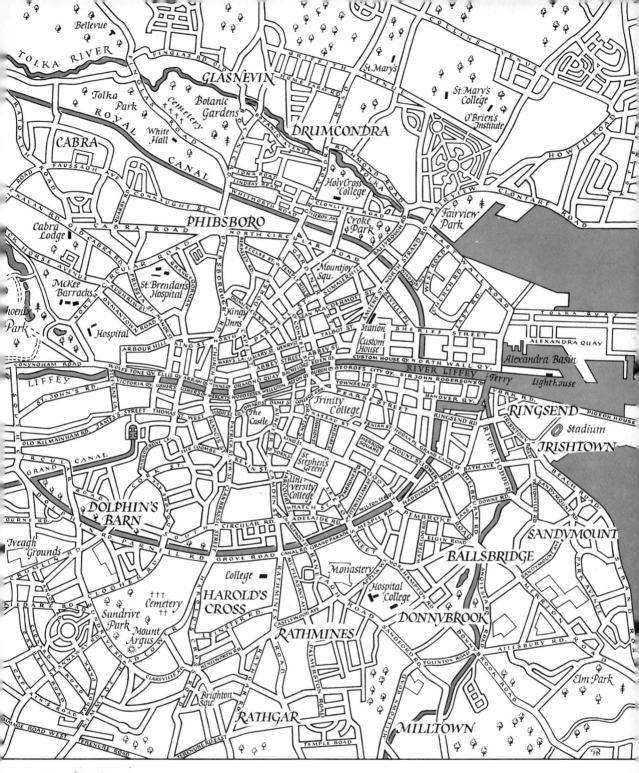

Map of Dublin.

Millbourne Lane, Drumcondra (*left*), near the Tolka River (*right*). 'He crossed the bridge over the stream of the Tolka and turned his eyes coldly for an instant towards the faded blue shrine of the Blessed Virgin which stood fowlwise on a pole in the middle of a hamshaped encampment of poor cottages.' (*A Portrait*)

Belvedere College   Joyce was an excellent student at Belvedere. In spite of the rising tides of disorder in his home life, he mastered Latin, French, Italian and arithmetic, and even Euclid and algebra. He did so well in English composition under the old-fashioned instruction of George Dempsey, a lay teacher called Mr Tate in the *Portrait*, that it might almost be said that he 'learned to write' at school.

But the family's plunge to poverty was accelerating. In February 1894, shortly after his twelfth birthday, Joyce accompanied his father to Cork, as Stephen accompanies his, to sell the last of the mortgaged properties. They stayed for a week in the Imperial Hotel (changed to the equally posh Victoria Hotel in the *Portrait*) and visited the scenes of John Joyce's youth – among them the anatomy theatre of Queen's College, where Joyce was embarrassed by the word FOETUS carved on a desk.

Since the money which father and son brought back to Dublin was owed to Reuben J. Dodd, a solicitor and money-lender satirized in *Ulysses*, the Joyce family was no better off than before. They moved again, to a smaller and poorer house in Millbourne Lane, Drumcondra, a working-class section of Dublin's north side near the Tolka River.

It was while they were in Millbourne Lane that Joyce was accused in class by Mr Dempsey of 'having heresy' in an essay; and that he was beaten by two classmates (called Heron and Boland in the *Portrait*) on his way home from school because he would not admit that Tennyson was a better poet than the immoral Byron. Like Stephen in the *Portrait*, Joyce (as Stanislaus substantiates) 'stumbled after them . . . clenching his fists madly and sobbing'. It was an

Joyce's homes at 29 Windsor Avenue (*left*) and 8 Royal Terrace (*right*). 'The lane behind the terrace was waterlogged and as he went down it slowly, choosing his steps amid heaps of wet rubbish, he heard a mad nun screeching in the nuns' madhouse beyond the wall – Jesus! O Jesus! Jesus!' (*A Portrait*)

important betrayal because this time the embryonic artist suffered for art and learned to surpass anger, hatred and love: 'Even that night as he stumbled homewards along Jones's Road he had felt that some power was divesting him of that sudden woven anger as easily as a fruit is divested of its soft ripe peel.'

From 1894 to 1897, Joyce briefly stimulated the family economy each spring by winning scholastic prizes. In 1897 he made his highest score, an exhibition prize of £30 a year for two years, for standing thirteenth in a group of forty-nine; to this was added a prize of £3 for the best English composition by anyone in Ireland in his grade. Joyce lent money to his impoverished family, took them to the theatre and to dinner, bought them gifts, and in general established a temporary tidy Scandinavia in his father's messy household. But the money was soon gone: 'The commonwealth fell, the loan bank closed its coffers and its books on a sensible loss, the rules of life which he [Stephen] had drawn about himself fell into desuetude.'

Late in 1894 the family moved back to the slightly better neighbourhood of Mountjoy Square, this time to 17 North Richmond Street, the 'blind' street of the story 'Araby'. They lived there four years, their longest sojourn anywhere since the early days at Bray. Living in the same street were several persons who, unbeknown to themselves, were becoming characters in Joyce's books: Eily and Eddie Boardman, combined as Edy Boardman in *Ulysses*; Ned Thornton, a tea-taster merged with John Joyce to form Mr Kernan in 'Grace' and *Ulysses*; his daughter Eveline, who gave her name and part of her personality to a *Dubliners* story; and others as well. Among Joyce's playmates were the boys who became Joe and Leo Dillon in 'An Encounter'; his brother Stanislaus, perhaps combined with little Alfred Bergan, Joyce's frequent companion on the long walks he liked to take in Dublin, became Mahoney in the same story.

Shoring these images and the quick cash of prizes against his ruin, Joyce was remembered chiefly during the next few years as being grave and studious while preparing for the next examination. He was also a pious boy and was admitted to the exclusive Sodality of the Blessed Virgin and, in 1896, elected its prefect, the highest student position in Belvedere College. But as 'An Encounter' suggests, he was also approaching precociously the end of his adolescence. That spring, at the age of fourteen, walking home from the theatre along the tree-lined path beside the Royal Canal, he met a prostitute and began his adult sexual life. Too young and of the wrong religion, the wrong social class and in the wrong century to become a roisterer, Joyce pursued for some years a furtive, guilt-ridden sexual life, finding continence, as he later told a friend, impossible. As he was to say of Stephen in the *Portrait*: 'His blood was in revolt. . . . He moaned to himself like some baffled prowling beast. He wanted to sin with another of his kind . . . and to exult with her in sin.' But 'On Saturday mornings when the sodality met in the chapel . . . he led his wing of boys through the responses. The falsehood of his position did not pain him.'

It did not pain him until November 1896, when Father James Cullen came to Belvedere from Clongowes to lead a retreat in honour of St Francis Xavier. Contemplating his bestiality and the 'smell of a horrible hell', Joyce in his shame and self-condemnation walked across North Dublin to confess to a Capuchin in Church Street Chapel, rather than to a Jesuit in Gardiner Street. He began to manage his prayers, mortifications and rituals with the same book-keeping enthusiasm he had given to the management of his prize-money.

During this spell of specious faith he impressed even his Jesuit teachers, who earlier had felt it necessary to warn his parents about his suspected immorality. They may have suggested, as the Director does to Stephen in the *Portrait*, that while listening for destiny's call, he listen for a vocation to the priesthood and to the Society of Jesus. But like Lucifer, Joyce felt the power of a single sin to undo all the piety of the past.

Joyce's more ordinary social life during his last two years at Belvedere included regular Sunday evening visits, often with Stanislaus, to the home of David Sheehy, MP, where the six Sheehy children arranged charades, games and singing for their guests. Joyce was popular for his wit and acting talent, and the group liked to hear him sing Irish, English and French songs in his fine tenor voice. Eugene and Richard Sheehy were also at Belvedere and Joyce was friendly with them as he was with their sisters. During those years, one of the sisters, Mary, became the object of his intense romantic love. Joyce had begun to think of himself as a poet, a conception which he never fully rejected. Some of the poems he wrote at this time were elicited by his feelings for Mary Sheehy. She may also have contributed to the character of the girl, unidentified in life, who became the Emma Clery of *Stephen Hero* and the *Portrait*, the 'lure of the fallen seraphim'.

Seraphim-Lucifer Joyce was about to fall again. 'He had not yet fallen but he would fall silently, in an instant. Not to fall was too hard, too hard.' He was not to fall with Mary, however, or any of the genteel young ladies he knew. He fell with a prostitute. In writing the *Portrait*, he moved the scene back to Millbourne Lane, probably to be able to include the Tolka and 'the faded blue shrine of the Blessed Virgin which stood fowlwise on a pole' and the 'faint sour stink of rotted cabbages . . . from the kitchen gardens. . . . He smiled to think that it was this disorder, the misrule and confusion of his father's house and the stagnation of vegetable life, which was to win the day in his soul.' Like Lucifer, Joyce fell in the faith, not from it. He watched it gradually 'fading down in his soul' until he felt the 'first noiseless sundering' of his life from that of his devout mother. He was ready to be converted to a new faith – a faith in mortal beauty.

This last conversion took place in the summer of 1898 as Joyce walked on Bull Island, off the Clontarf shore in Dublin Bay. He saw a girl wading in the tidal stream, 'one whom magic had changed into the likeness of a strange and beautiful seabird', but who was really an 'angel of mortal youth and beauty, an envoy from the fair courts of life' sent 'to throw open before him in an instant of ecstasy the gates of all the ways of error and glory'. It was the destined moment of rebirth and transfiguration which his 'mythy' mind had foreseen. Like Stephen in the *Portrait* he felt that 'his soul had arisen from the grave of boyhood', and to 'the call of life to his soul' he answered: 'Yes! Yes! Yes! He would create proudly out of the freedom and power of his soul . . . a living thing . . . imperishable.'

A new man, he enrolled that autumn at University College, Dublin, the belated and tawdry consequence of Newman's 'Idea of a University'. Joyce was no longer the docile student he had been. Even during his last year at Belvedere his results in the national examinations were less good, his attendance had become irregular and he had indulged his impishness by 'taking off' Father

University College, Dublin

University College, Dublin (UCD), in St Stephen's Green.

25

Henrik Ibsen, a lithograph by Edvard Munch, 1902.

Henry, the Rector, when he played the part of Dr Grimstone, the buffoonish schoolmaster in Anstey's *Vice Versa*, a play about the magical metamorphosis of a father into the physical likeness of his son, and vice versa. At University College he was inattentive during lectures, frequently late for them and sometimes absent. He engaged in horseplay and practical jokes. He stopped washing his body, wryly enjoying his lice. His rebellion reached a minor climax in the spring of 1899, when he refused to sign a popular protest against Yeats's *The Countess Cathleen* following its production at the opening of the National Literary Theatre.

Fortunately, to feed his rebellion he continued his avid reading and his study of Italian, French, German and Latin. To these he added literary Norwegian so that he could read Ibsen and write to him – the rebel who said that 'to live is to war with the trolls' and that he would 'torpedo the ark', a phrase which Joyce echoes in *Stephen Hero*. With equal enthusiasm he also read Dante, D'Annunzio, Giordano Bruno, Flaubert and Hauptmann. Encouraged by Father Charles Ghezzi, his Italian teacher (who appears under his own name in the *Portrait* and in *Ulysses* and as Almidano Artifoni, a real person in Trieste whom Joyce had yet to meet), he began to compound from their ideas and from those of Aristotle, Aquinas, Shelley, Coleridge and Wilde the aesthetic theory which he presented to his fellow-students in a paper called 'Drama and Life'. He read his paper on 20 January 1900 to the UCD Literary and Historical Society, an organization which, with the National Library, formed the centre of Dublin intellectual life. Joyce argued for 'real life on the stage' as if he were Zola. But his naturalism was tempered by symbolism, for he sounded, too, like Shelley and Blake, finding the universal and mythical in the real events of everyday modern life:

> *Ghosts*, the action of which passes in a common parlour, is of universal import – a deepset branch on the tree Igdrasil, whose roots are stuck in earth, but through whose higher leafage the stars of heaven are glowing and astir.

In April 1900, Joyce followed up the success of his paper by publishing in *The Fortnightly Review* an article called 'Ibsen's New Drama'. This article launched him, at the age of eighteen, on his public career as a writer. Besides bringing him twelve guineas, it brought forth a response from the old Master Builder himself, who sent Joyce a message of thanks through his English translator William Archer.

A later reprint of Joyce's early article on Ibsen.

James Joyce (*at right*) with his University College friends George Clancy and J.F.Byrne.

College Friends   Joyce's friends during his UCD days included J.F.Byrne (Cranly in the *Portrait*), George Clancy (Davin), Francis Skeffington (McCann), Vincent Cosgrave (Lynch), Constantine P.Curran (Donovan) and Thomas Kettle, who shows up under his own name in *Finnegans Wake*. Clancy represented athletic Irish Nationalism, Skeffington modern liberal nationalism, Cosgrave cynical atheism, Curran accommodation and Kettle the Europeanization of Ireland. But it was to J.F.Byrne that Joyce 'poured out his soul night after night' as he adjusted his life to his rejection of Catholicism and his new aims as 'a priest of eternal imagination'. And it was Byrne, Cosgrave and, later, Oliver St John Gogarty, whom Joyce was to see as his sombre or gay betrayers, trying to sacrifice his new spiritual orientation on their respective altars of materialism, compromise and sexual triumph.

Joyce came to regard a number of his UCD teachers as obtuse and cliché-ridden men. In the *Portrait* he concentrates this disgust in the sententious Dean of Studies with whom Stephen, using the Dean's own weapon – Aquinian distinctions between the Beautiful and the Good – fences triumphantly before the fireplace of the physics theatre.

The Joyce family had moved several more times on Dublin's north side – to 29 Windsor Avenue, Fairview, late in 1898; to 13 Richmond Avenue, Fairview, in 1899; and to 8 Royal Terrace in 1900. It is at this last address that Stephen is living at the opening of Chapter Five of the *Portrait*, where his role as levite of the imagination, so overblown at the end of Chapter Four, is punctured with irony as he chews eucharistic crusts of fried bread and plays with a tin of the family's pawn-tickets, observing their louse-marks. After allowing his mother to perform ineffectual ablutions on him, Stephen heads for the University. He crosses the bridge over the Royal Canal on the North Strand Road where the narrator waits for Mahoney in 'An Encounter', walks up Talbot Place past I. Downes's cake-shop to O'Connell Street and Nelson's Pillar. There he turns left and walks southward towards the Liffey, past the statues of Sir John Gray and Daniel O'Connell at Hopkins' corner. Crossing O'Connell Bridge, Stephen sees the 'grimy marine-dealer's shop'. Joyce might also have seen the Scotch House (with Mulligan's in Poolbeg Street, one of Farrington's drunken stops in 'Counterparts') farther on the left, the Ballast House dead ahead (even the Ballast House clock, most prosaic of time-pieces, was 'capable of an epiphany'), and to the right, George Webb's book-stalls on Aston Quay. He passes the grey block of Trinity College at the foot of Grafton Street and the 'droll statue of the national poet of Ireland', Thomas Moore, finally reaching St Stephen's Green and the UCD buildings where, having missed his morning classes, but having thought intently on Ibsen, Newman, Hauptmann, Guido Cavalcanti and his University friends, he discovers the Dean of Studies lighting the fire in the physics theatre.

Fireplace in the Physics Theatre, UCD. 'A figure was crouching before the large grate and by its leanness and greyness he knew that it was the dean of studies lighting the fire.' (*A Portrait*)

Mulligan's in Poolbeg Street.

O'Connell Bridge at Hopkins' Corner.

Statue of Thomas Moore (*left centre*) and the Examination Hall of Trinity College (*left*).

St Stephen's Green. '. . . they crossed the street and began to walk round the enclosure inside the chains. A few mechanics and their sweethearts were sitting on the swinging chains turning the shadows to account.' (*Stephen Hero*)

Grafton Street, 'gay with housed awnings lured [Bloom's] senses. Muslin prints silk, dames and dowagers, jingle of harnesses, hoofthuds lowringing in the baking causeway.' (*Ulysses*)

Max Beerbohm's comment on Archer and Ibsen.

Eleonora Duse.

Joyce, like Stephen, was beginning to scale heights of consciousness where his family, his fellow-students and his teachers could not follow him. Because of his reading in European literature, his gradual mastery of languages, Ibsen's notice of him, and his own visit to London with his father in the spring of 1900, paid for by his *Fortnightly Review* article, he began to think of himself as a European rather than an Irishman. In London he and his father had seen D'Annunzio's mistress, the great Eleanora Duse, act, and Joyce had demanded and received the attention of William Archer, Ibsen's translator.

His orientation towards Europe was confirmed in the summers of 1900 and 1901, when he and his father stayed in Mullingar. Joyce shocked the residents of the country market-town by statements like 'My mind is more interesting to me than the entire country.' During the first summer he wrote a play, *A Brilliant Career*, which he called the 'first true work of my life' and which he dedicated to his 'own soul' though he later had the good sense to destroy it; during the second summer he translated Hauptmann's *Vor Sonnenaufgang* and *Michael Kramer*.

In this race towards the summit, Joyce saw himself outdistancing not only contemporaries and mentors, but also the established writers of the Irish Literary

George Russell (AE).   Lady Gregory.   W.B. Yeats.

Revival – W.B. Yeats, George Russell (AE), John Synge, Lady Gregory, George Moore, Padraic Colum, Edward Martyn and the rest. He thought the Revival was looking backwards. Abandoning his Gaelic lessons, he wrote an article which he called 'The Day of the Rabblement', damning the provincialism of the Revival and declaring his isolation from the Irish multitude and his alliance with Bruno and Ibsen:

No man, said the Nolan, can be a lover of the true or the good unless he abhors the multitude; and the artist, though he may employ the crowd, is very careful to isolate himself.

He proclaimed Hauptmann Ibsen's heir and saw himself waiting to enter the throne room when his hour came. 'Even now,' he concluded, 'that hour may be standing by the door.'

When Joyce submitted this article to *St Stephen's*, the college magazine, he had his first experience of censorship. As at Clongowes, he took his case to the ultimate authority, Father William Delaney, the President, but this time without success. An article by Francis Skeffington calling for equal status for women in the University had also been rejected by *St Stephen's*, so the two men

33

published the articles together privately, and peddled them among the Dublin intelligentsia.

During his University days Joyce wrote many poems, illustrating moods of gaiety and sadness; he gathered them in manuscript books called *Moods* and *Shine and Dark*. The few that survive suggest odes to Stephen Dowling Botts:

> *Yea, for this love of mine*
> *I have given all I had;*
> *For she was passing fair,*
> *And I was passing mad.*
>
> *All flesh, it is said,*
> *Shall wither as the grass;*
> *The fuel for the oven*
> *Shall be consumed, alas!*

He also began to write brief prose sketches – dialogues, interior monologues, reports of dreams and images of the life of the spirit – which he called 'epiphanies'. The term meant both a 'showing forth' or 'revelation of the whatness' by a thing, and the moment of poetic apprehension, when a thing is seen as 'that thing which it is and no other thing'. In 1902, Joyce read some of the epiphanies to Yeats, who called them 'a beautiful though immature and eccentric harmony of little prose descriptions and meditations'. Joyce told Yeats that he had 'thrown over metrical form . . . that he might get a form so fluent that it would respond to the motions of the spirit', a notion which he was to repeat in the essay 'Portrait' of 1904, in which he first used epiphanies in a longer work. On this same occasion he criticized Yeats severely (and by implication the entire Irish Literary Revival) for his concern with politics, the historical setting of events, ideas, and especially folk-lore, saying, according to Yeats, that 'his own mind . . . was much nearer to God than folk-lore [was]'.

Although the epiphanies which survive are slight enough, some of them proved effective when 'placed' in longer works. Their rich complexity and compression help to justify the high value which the youthful Joyce placed on them, though he satirized his evaluation in *Ulysses*:

> Remember your epiphanies on green oval leaves, deeply deep, copies to be sent if you died to all the great libraries of the world, including Alexandria? Someone was to read them there after a few thousand years, a mahamanvantara.

But in spite of his later irony towards his youth, Joyce also realized that in the epiphanies, with their careful attention to details drawn from life, their selective process of letting all but the essentials drop out of the scene, the detachment of their dramatic form, and the careful ordering of their parts, he was beginning to learn his art. Unable to write plays – as he would demonstrate again in 1915 by writing *Exiles* – he was able to write completely dramatic narrative fiction: 'The Sisters' by 1904, 'An Encounter' by 1905 and the Christmas dinner scene in the *Portrait* by 1909.

The family moved again, to 32 Glengariff Parade in 1901 and then, in 1902, to 7 St Peter's Terrace, Cabra, the last house they were to occupy while Joyce remained in Dublin. To buy this house John Joyce commuted half his small pension. Joyce, having completed the work for his Bachelor's degree in the summer of 1902, was by then attending St Cecilia's Medical School. But there was now so little money at home that none could be spared to pay his fees. On an impulse he decided to go to Paris to study medicine at the Sorbonne.

He wrote to Lady Gregory, to whom Yeats had introduced him, explaining that he was leaving Dublin 'alone and friendless' and re-asserting his 'faith in the soul, which changes all things and fills their inconstancy with light'. 'I want to achieve myself,' he said, 'little or great as I may be – for I know that there is no heresy or no philosophy which is so abhorrent to my church as a human being.' Lady Gregory replied advising him to take some warm clothes and helped him to get some books to review for the *Daily Express*. She also wrote to Yeats, who invited Joyce to stop with him in London.

Joyce in his graduation robes and in a UCD graduation group (*second from left*). 'Mother is putting my new secondhand clothes in order. She prays now, she says, that I may learn in my own life and away from home and friends what the heart is and what it feels. Amen.' (*A Portrait*)

The Liffey, from the North Wall.

Arthur W. Symons.

Foot of the Eiffel Tower, Paris.

Joyce left Dublin from the North Wall (where Eveline found that she could not make herself board the ship) on the evening of 1 December 1902. Yeats, who had overlooked Joyce's early brashness, met him at Euston Station and found him 'unexpectedly amiable'. He fed Joyce, introduced him at the offices of the *Academy* and the *Speaker*, and in the evening took him to see Arthur Symons. Symons was to prove helpful, by placing some of Joyce's poems in periodicals and helping him, four years later, to publish *Chamber Music*, his first book.

That night Joyce went to Paris. He saw himself soaring, like a successful Icarus, out of the labyrinth of Dublin into exciting, unknown worlds. But he needed also to feel betrayed and exiled. More of a trip than a journey, this first visit to the Continent lasted only long enough for Joyce to attend a few classes

First Trips to Paris

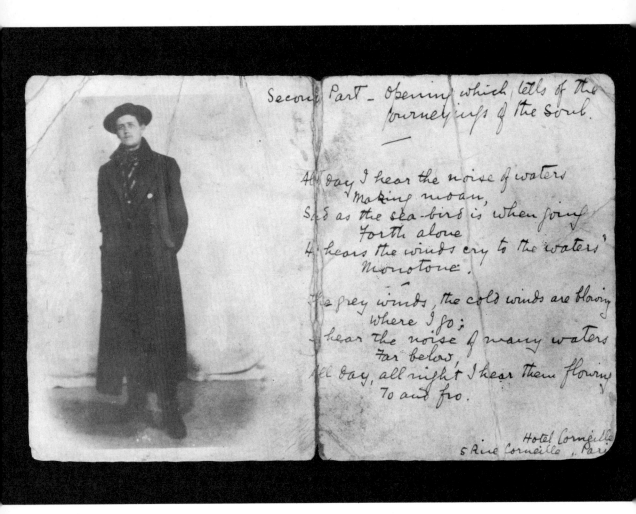

Postcard with photograph and poem which

at the École de Médecine and to dream of future possibilities before writing home for his fare to return to Dublin for Christmas.

Two of the letters his mother wrote to him in Paris during this two-week flight from the parental nest suggest their relationship. She wrote epiphanies of mother-love: 'I only wish I was near you to look after and comfort you.' And ego-feeding apologies: 'My dear Jim if you are disappointed in my letter and if as usual I fail to understand what you would wish to explain, believe me it is

Photo-Cartes, 28, 1st Poissonnière, Paris.

CARTE POSTALE

Ce côté est exclusivement reservé à l'adresse.

Please forward

@ M John F Byrne
20 East Essex St
Dublin
Ireland.

Joyce sent from Paris, during his first trip there in 1902, to J. F. Byrne.

not from any want of longing desire to do so . . . but as you so often said I am stupid and cannot grasp the great thoughts which are yours.'

Sure of the money for his ticket home and exhilarated at the prospect of returning to Dublin, Joyce visited a theatre, a brothel and a photographer's studio, where he was snapped in an outsized overcoat looking like a Monte Cristo who just might not return. He sent a photo-postcard of himself to Byrne, on which he wrote a new poem, 'Second Part – opening which tells of the

Toulouse-Lautrec's painting of a Paris brothel: *Au Salon, rue des Moulins*, 1895.

journeyings of the soul', and one to Cosgrave, describing in dog-Latin his adventures with Paris prostitutes. It was for such Dionysian exploits that Joyce was to tell Stanislaus that the government should give him a pension, because he knew how to live. When Cosgrave showed Byrne his postcard, it became one cause of the estrangement between Joyce and Byrne.

Discovering Byrne's coolness on his return to Dublin just before Christmas, Joyce was baffled. But he knew there had to be a Tim Healy somewhere, for his books as well as his life, and he imagined Byrne as desiring to steal his Emma and to pervert his aims as an artist by tempting him to lead a materialistic life. In *Stephen Hero* it is Cranly who urges Stephen to become a butcher and use his love-poems to wrap up pork sausages.

As a new betrayer Joyce found Oliver St John Gogarty, home from his studies at Oxford, who as Buck Mulligan in *Ulysses* is compared to Cranly in many ways. Unlike Byrne, however, Gogarty was obscene, blasphemous, witty, talented, rich, and well on his way to succeeding in Joyce's ambition of combining the careers of medicine and writing.

Joyce stayed almost a month in Dublin. He visited the Sheehys, spent much of his time at the National Library, and learned from Gogarty how to carouse. At the Library he spoke again to T. W. Lyster, the Director, and met Richard A. Best and W. K. Magee (who wrote as 'John Eglinton') – all members of the staff who appear in *Ulysses*.

On his way back to Paris he stopped in London to burnish the contacts made earlier through Yeats. He called again on William Archer, met Lady Gregory and just missed meeting John Synge.

In Paris he spent most of his days in the Bibliothèque Nationale, his nights in the Bibliothèque Sainte-Geneviève, reading Ben Jonson and Aristotle, and

Reading room of the National Library, Dublin. 'Cranly was sitting over near the dictionaries. A thick book, opened at the frontispiece, lay before him on the wooden rest.' (*A Portrait*)

Reading room of the Bibliothèque Nationale, Paris.

writing the 'dagger definitions' of aesthetic terms which Stephen, improving on
Aristotle and Aquinas, expounds to Lynch in the *Portrait*. Within a few
weeks he also wrote two of his best poems – 'I hear an army charging upon
the land' and 'When the shy star goes forth in heaven' – as well as fifteen more
epiphanies. He reaffirmed his rejection of the 'cultic twalette' and his resolution
to be his own man:

> And so help me devil I will write only the things that approve themselves
> to me. . . . So damn Russell, damn Yeats, damn Skeffington, damn
> Darlington, damn editors, damn free-thinkers, damn vegetable verse and
> double damn vegetable philosophy!

Bibliothèque Sainte-Geneviève, Paris: the reading room.

Entrance to the Bibliothèque Nationale and exterior of the Bibliothèque Sainte-Geneviève.

At the end of two months he outlined for his mother the time-table for the next fifteen years of his life:

> My book of songs will be published in the spring of 1907. My first comedy about five years later. My 'Esthetic' about five years later again. (This *must* interest you!)

In general, Joyce stuck to the schedule, gradually revealing himself as a writer of remarkable perseverance as well as genius.

Living at the Hôtel Corneille, where he had stayed on his first trip to Paris, Joyce met John Synge near there, walking the streets to save his coal. Synge had the beginning of the end of *his* struggle for recognition as a writer in his travelling-bag – the manuscript of *Riders to the Sea*. Joyce read it, 'riddling it mentally', as he wrote Stanislaus, cleverly pointing out to Synge its departures from Aristotle's canons in magnitude and in the cause of the catastrophe, much as he had deprecated the work of other fellow-Irishmen. Nevertheless, his defences secure, he learned the final speeches of Maurya by heart, as he had the final speech of Yeats's *Cathleen*. A few years later he translated the play into Italian and helped to produce it in English.

Joyce met two other Irishmen in Paris – Joseph Casey, a former Fenian, who became Kevin Egan in *Ulysses*, and his estranged son, Patrice, who appears under his own name. Joyce borrowed money as well as their personalities from them. He also wrote some book reviews for the *Daily Express*, and sold to the *Irish Times* a barbed jab at an age of technology in the form of an interview with a French racing driver. He re-used the material in the *Dubliners* story 'After the Race'. By these and other expedients, Joyce prospered in Paris until Good Friday, 1903, when he received a cable from Dublin: 'MOTHER DYING COME HOME FATHER.'

Dublin Again His mother was dying of cancer. As she wept and vomited the green bile which Stephen recalls in *Ulysses*, she begged him to make his Easter Duties by confessing his sins, doing penance and receiving Holy Communion. With reluctance and feelings of guilt Joyce refused. His favourite Aunt Josephine, and Byrne, with whom he had become somewhat reconciled, expostulated with him, but his apostasy was fixed. Although he continued to admire the drama of the Roman ritual and even to attend certain services during Holy Week each year, he had 'secularized' it. On Holy Thursday, the night before his father's telegram arrived, he had attended the Good Friday *Tenebrae* service in Notre-Dame; the notes he made on that occasion make a shadowy appearance in the last chapter of the *Portrait*, and contribute to the 'monomyth' of *Finnegans Wake*.

O'Meara's Irish House, Dublin.
The statue in the second arched niche is
of Daniel O'Connell.

Goliard Joyce, dressed in his Latin-Quarter hat and wide Paris tie, sought solace in the company of Gogarty, Cosgrave and another medical student, John Elwood, who is Temple in the *Portrait*. They continued his instruction in the Dublin habit of regular drinking, which he pursued through the rest of his life.

Stanislaus, too, became a frequent companion: the whetstone on which the lancet of Joyce's art was sharpened, not least by the gritty kernels of fact Stanislaus gave him for such *Dubliners* stories as 'A Painful Case', 'Grace', and 'Ivy Day in the Committee Room'. His brother was also a handy, appreciative, though intelligently critical audience on whom Joyce depended for another decade and more.

Among the Dublin literary establishment Lady Gregory and George Moore snubbed Joyce. He affected disdain for their opinions, but Padraic Colum, who did not snub him, was rewarded with similar disdain and a contempt which continued until they renewed their acquaintance during the 1920s.

For four months Joyce watched his mother die. She died on 13 August 1903, aged forty-four, two days before the Feast of the Assumption of the Blessed Virgin. In the last week Joyce sang Yeats's 'Who Goes with Fergus?' for her. He was obliged to lock up his drunken father in another room when he screamed to his wife that she should 'Die and be damned'. But he refused, as Stanislaus had, his Uncle John Murray's demand that he kneel to pray during her last hours. The guilt he felt at this refusal, combined with that he felt over his refusal to make his Easter Duties, formed the 'agenbite of inwit' which followed him after May Joyce had been laid in Glasnevin Cemetery, as it follows Stephen in *Ulysses*:

> In a dream, silently, she had come to him, her wasted body within its loose graveclothes giving off an odour of wax and rosewood . . . a faint odour of wetted ashes.
>
> Her glazing eyes, staring out of death, to shake and bend my soul. On me alone. The ghostcandle to light her agony. Ghostly light on the tortured face. Her hoarse loud breath rattling in horror, while all prayed on their knees. Her eyes on me to strike me down. *Liliata rutilantium te confessorum.* . . .

Joyce hung around Dublin all that autumn. He read a good deal and wrote nineteen book reviews for the *Daily Express* before he was fired. He applied unsuccessfully for a job in the National Library. Through Skeffington, who had become UCD Registrar, he was offered some evening classes in French, but he declined the offer to the Dean, Father Darlington, saying that his French was not good enough. He attended a few law classes and some medical classes at St Cecilia's. He turned to pawning articles and books. He found some solace for his frustrations in socialism, anarchism, and the philosophy of Nietzsche, which confirmed one of his masks of cold selfishness and indifferent licentiousness, as well as deepening his belief in the importance of the redemptive ego choosing in 'this moment'.

After his wife's early death John Joyce became a steady drunkard and a man of some cruelty. He grudged the money his daughter Margaret, who had taken over the housekeeping, needed for food and gave her too little if she asked for it when he was on his way to the pub. According to Stanislaus, he was capable of saying after refusing money for food, 'I'll break your bloody heart! . . . I'll break your stomach first though, ye buggers.' And according to *Ulysses*, 'I'll leave you where Jesus left the jews.'

The Grand Canal, from the Baggot Street Bridge.

Dame Street, leading to Trinity College.

Joyce, however, in spite of his indolence and his grasping for funds, was approaching his adult life as a writer. On 7 January 1904, in a copybook belonging to his sister Mabel, he wrote an autobiographical essay-story, at once romantic and ironic, which he called 'A Portrait of the Artist'. He submitted the story to *Dana*, a new magazine edited by John Eglinton. When it was rejected, Joyce immediately began to turn it into *Stephen Hero* and then, ten years later, into *A Portrait of the Artist as a Young Man*, which preserves the idea of the early story – to present the past without nostalgia as a 'fluid succession of presents' which do not wear an 'iron memorial aspect' but show 'the features of infancy . . . in the adolescent portrait.'

Though he took time off for carousing with Gogarty, for visits to Nighttown, for a walk to the Dublin mountains with Mary Sheehy and others, and for the writing of some of the poems which became part of *Chamber Music*, Joyce worked steadily at *Stephen Hero*, finishing the first chapter by 10 February. To the consternation of Gogarty and other friends, he had begun to convert his life directly into fiction, turning from their company to jot down notes and epiphanies on the library slips he now carried with him.

In March, he again thought of making a career as a singer. Encouraged by John McCormack, he took lessons and entered the Feis Ceoil ('fish coil', as Dubliners say) in May. He sang the set pieces so well that the judge was prepared to award him the gold medal, but when Joyce refused to sing at sight, he was given a second-class medal instead.

Joyce then turned to teaching, and was employed at the Clifton School for boys on the Vico Road in Dalkey, a southern suburb of Dublin, for a few weeks – long enough to give him the experience which he used in the second episode of *Ulysses*.

During the spring of 1904 he had several singing engagements in Dublin. Still the gay goliard, he now conceived the plan of combining a visit to Gogarty at Oxford with a singing tour of English resort towns, the lute on which he hoped to accompany himself to be provided by Arnold Dolmetsch, trousers and funds by Gogarty. Dolmetsch and Gogarty discouraged him in this.

Nora Barnacle   In June, however, he did receive some encouragement. Walking down budding Nassau Street in his yachting cap and canvas shoes, he met Nora Barnacle, a tall, brown-haired girl from Galway, and fell in love. She was a simple, proud, outspoken country girl who had recently come to Dublin, where she had found work as a chambermaid in Finn's Hotel. Misled by Joyce's well-known costume (Stephen wears it in *Ulysses*), Nora mistook him for a sailor – a Nassau Street version, perhaps, of Nausicaa's Ulysses.

They met on 10 June. On the evening of 16 June they went walking at Ringsend where, nine years before, the child Joyce, within sight of the Pigeon

Nassau Street. '[Bloom] crossed at Nassau street corner and stood before the window of Yeates and Son, pricing the field glasses.' (*Ulysses*)

House but unable to reach it, had encountered the pervert. It was that day, as Joyce later told Nora, 'you made me a man'. A decade and a half later the day became 'Bloomsday', the day on which *Ulysses* takes place, the day on which callow, overweening Dedalus learns what love means: 'the desire of good for another', as Joyce says in his notes for *Exiles*, his most direct meditation on the relationship between himself and Nora.

Nora gave Joyce many of the qualities he needed in a woman: faithfulness, trust, tenderness, dominance, wit. She combined innocence and earthiness in

proportions that nearly fulfilled his longing for purity and desecration: he recalled their encounter on 16 June as 'a sacrament which left in me a final sense of sorrow and degradation'. She was maternal enough to play Rhea to his Zeus, paternal enough to play Circe to his swine, unformed enough to be his Galatea, faithful enough to be his Penelope. She provided the 'reality of experience' which helped him form Gretta Conroy in 'The Dead', Bertha Rowan in *Exiles*, Molly Bloom in *Ulysses* and Anna Livia Plurabelle in *Finnegans Wake*. The only roles she could not play were those of intellectual companion – a bit-part which Joyce continued to fill for himself with the help of understudies like Gogarty, Cosgrave and Curran – and of betrayer, an essential part that Joyce invented for her, five years after their first meeting.

Nora Barnacle Joyce, '... your soul seems to me to be the most beautiful and simple soul in the world.' (*Letters*)

60 Shelbourne Road

I may be blind. I looked for a long time at a head of reddish-brown hair and decided it was not yours. I went home quite dejected. I would like to make an appointment but it might not suit you. I hope you will be kind enough to make one with me — if you have not forgotten me!

15 June 1904   James A Joyce

One of Joyce's first letters to Nora.

A letter from Nora to Joyce.

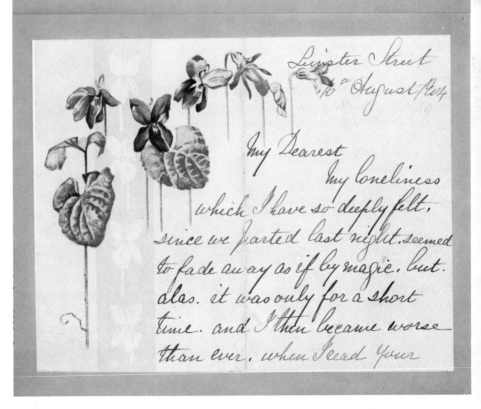

Leinster Street
16° August 1904

My Dearest
            My loneliness which I have so deeply felt, since we parted last night. seemed to fade away as if by magic. but. alas. it was only for a short time. and I then became worse than ever. when I read your

While his love matured, Joyce lived through the drunken summer on hospitality and small loans from various hands. When George Russell (AE) asked him in July for a short story for the *Irish Homestead*, for a guinea Joyce quickly wrote 'The Sisters', signing it 'Stephen Daedalus' because he was ashamed to have his aristocratic name appear in the publication known in Dublin as 'the pigs' paper'. His designing imagination, however, immediately conceived of 'The Sisters' as the first of 'a series of epicleti – ten' which he already called *Dubliners* 'to betray the soul of that hemiplegia or paralysis which many consider a city'. *Epicleti* referred to the prayer of the Orthodox Church in which the Holy Ghost is invoked to transmute bread and wine into the body and blood of Christ. He saw himself giving people, as he told Stanislaus, 'some kind of intellectual pleasure or spiritual enjoyment by converting the bread of every-day life into something that has a permanent artistic life of its own'. His approach to *Dubliners* was already complete – to show forth, in a style of 'scrupulous meanness' what he called 'the significance of trivial things' and the paralytic subservience of Dubliners to family, Church and State.

By the autumn, Joyce had written two more stories for the *Homestead*, 'Eveline' and 'After the Race'. They represented a great creative advance over *Stephen Hero*, which he continued to work on. If these stories with their combination of realism and symbolism in an open-ended form seem less original now than they did then, it is only because Joyce and Chekhov arrived almost simultaneously at similar techniques which gave the modern short story its main line of development. They were original, too, in their 'mimetic style', the meanness of which helped to present non-discursively the meanness of the city and its citizens. Joyce had experimented with the stylistic imitation of life in some of his epiphanies and in the essay 'Portrait' of 1904. The style came to quick fruition in 'The Sisters' with the presentation of the deceased paralytic, Father Flynn, in the paralyzed minds of his bromidic survivors.

The mimetic style is one of Joyce's accomplishments. If he cannot be said to have invented it, he can nevertheless be held its greatest practitioner. In Joyce's work it is a conspiracy of sentence patterns, imagery and action which expresses not the sound of the subject but of the object – not the sound of the author's voice but of the character's voice and thoughts and feelings. He would soon extend the range of objects presented to include machinery, rivers, sticks and stones. In *Finnegans Wake*, for instance, as darkness falls and distance grows and the narrator turns into a tree, he says:

can't hear with the waters of. The chittering waters of. Flittering bats, field-mice bawk talk. Ho! Are you not gone ahome? What Thom Malone? Can't hear with bawk of bats, all them liffeying waters of. Ho, talk save us. My foos won't moos. I feel as old as yonder elm.

Joyce in 1904.

Title-page of *Chamber Music*,
Joyce's first collection of
poems, published in 1907.

'Chamber Music'

In spite of this new start in prose, Joyce continued to think of himself as a poet, a notion encouraged by the acceptance of five of his poems in 1904 by the *Speaker, Dana*, and *The Venture*. He had begun to call his manuscript collection of poems 'Chamber Music' at the suggestion of Stanislaus; many of them were slight lyrics in the Jacobean mode he admired, meant to be sung by a lover. The title was given an appropriate twist that summer when Joyce and Gogarty took his manuscript – one poem to each parchment sheet – to read aloud to a gay widow called Jenny. They had also brought some Guinness, which soon caused the widow to use her chamber-pot behind a screen. As they listened to her go to pot, Gogarty acclaimed her as a critic and Joyce applauded his choice of title, no doubt aware that many of the poems were susceptible of interpretations relating not only to their musical quality, but also to their imagery of micturition, chambering and the false wantonness of onanism. They were, as he said in *Finnegans Wake*, 'shamebred music'.

Strings in the earth and air
Make music sweet;
Strings by the river where
The willows meet.

There's music along the river
For love wanders there,
Pale flowers on his mantle,
Dark leaves on his hair.

All softly playing,
With head to the music bent,
And fingers straying
Upon an instrument.

It was during this summer that he wrote his broadside blast, 'The Holy Office', in which he appraised in his favour the relative worth of the 'mumming company' of the writers of the Irish Literary Revival and himself. They were parochial servitors of Mammon and 'the rabblement', he a proud, antler-flashing exile following witty Aristotle and steely Aquinas to the world summits:

Where they have crouched and crawled and prayed
I stand, the self-doomed, unafraid,
Unfellowed, friendless and alone,
Indifferent as the herring-bone,
Firm as the mountain ridges where
I flash my antlers on the air.

He had 'The Holy Office' printed in Dublin, but the copies were not delivered immediately because the printer demanded payment in cash.

As the broadside suggests, Joyce was preparing again to take his soul into exile. Only Nora bound him to Dublin. He had not lived with his family since shortly after his mother's death. He told Nora late in August that his mother had been 'slowly killed . . . by my father's ill-treatment, by years of trouble, and by my cynical frankness of conduct'. He 'cursed the system which had made her a victim' and felt that his brothers and sisters were 'nothing' to him. Like other heroes, as the *Portrait* implies, he was psychologically andro-gynous and begotten not made, 'fosterchild and fosterbrother'. He had left 'Mother Church' six years before 'hating it fervently' and now making 'open war upon it'.

Sandycove (*above*) and the Martello Tower (*right*) where Joyce lived briefly in September 1904 and where he set the opening chapter of *Ulysses*.

On 7 September, while marking time before his departure, he set up house‑keeping with Gogarty and Samuel Trench (an Anglo‑Irish enthusiast for the Irish revival) in the Martello Tower, Sandycove, where he domiciled Stephen in *Ulysses*. It was during his two weeks there that he proposed to Nora that they leave Ireland together and share a 'hazardous life'.

Nora agreed and Joyce set about borrowing their fare. He had received assurances, through an English agent, of a place teaching at the Berlitz Language School in Zürich. He left Dublin with Nora from the North Wall on 9 October, and borrowed more money in Paris to get to Zürich, where they arrived on 11 October. Full of fears and hopes, they consummated their elope‑ment in the Gasthaus Hoffnung, since demolished to make way for the main railway transfer depot of the Zürich Post Office.

Pola. The Berlitz building next to the Arch of Sergius, via Giulia (now Laginje) and via Medolino, where Joyce worked and lived.

The Berlitz officials knew nothing of the agent who had promised Joyce a job in Zürich. They sent him on to Trieste, where there was no opening either. While he waited for something to turn up, he wrote another chapter of *Stephen Hero* and began a story about the family of his Uncle William Murray which became 'Clay'. Finally, the Berlitz director, Almidano Artifoni, whose name *Pola* Joyce gave to Father Ghezzi in *Ulysses*, found him a place in Pola, 'a naval Siberia', as Joyce called it, down the Adriatic coast at the tip of the Istrian peninsula.

The couple moved into a furnished room at 2 via Giulia, just round the corner from the Berlitz School, which occupied quarters next to the Roman Arch of Sergius at the south-west end of the city square. It was Joyce's first opportunity to compare Roman ruins with ruined Ireland. Pola offered not only the arch and street, but also a large and almost intact amphitheatre, fortifications and a theatre. His sense of the past and of the rise and fall of civilizations, which he was to employ so thoroughly in *Finnegans Wake*, must have been heightened, too, by the polyglot quality of Pola, where Italian and German were super-imposed on Serbo-Croatian tongues.

Joyce and Nora were poor and lonely in Pola, a sleepy backwater, though they made durable friendships with Alessandro Francini Bruni and his wife, and more temporary relationships with other teachers at the Scuola Berlitz. Francini, a Florentine, improved Joyce's Italian by teaching him pure Tuscan. Joyce continued to write *Stephen Hero* and kept a notebook of Aquinian distinctions. Nora became pregnant and the stoveless flat grew cold, but Joyce finished four more chapters of *Stephen Hero*. In January they moved into Francini's house where they had a larger room with a stove and even a desk. Nora studied French in the hope that the novel would sell and become their ticket to Paris.

Joyce sent the first fourteen chapters to Stanislaus for appreciation and criticism. When the criticism arrived, the lancet spurned the whetstone. He also complained to Stanislaus of his 'worse than solitude of the intellect' and told him that he was wearing pince-nez with a very strong prescription.

While he wrote in Pola Joyce also read: socialist pamphlets, Renan's *Souvenirs* and *Vie de Jésus*, novels and stories by Henry James, Tolstoy, George Moore, Conan Doyle, and Marie Corelli's *Sorrows of Satan*. He kept writing to Stanislaus asking him to send more books and to come out himself to join them, arguing that a career could be built there on fine clothes and a moustache.

He grew a moustache himself and curled his hair with Nora's curling-iron, the first stage of a continuing dandyism, and he had some of his decayed teeth filled. He bought a new suit and a pork-pie hat and had himself photographed

The Temple of Augustus and an Italian Renaissance house in Pola.

Pola. The harbour and amphitheatre. 'Pola is a back-of-God-speed place – a naval Siberia.' (*Letters*)

in them. He hired a piano and sang his way through the winter, hoping he could get out of Austria into Italy by the summer. He did not have to wait so long: he and Nora, along with the other aliens, were expelled from Pola in March, when a spy ring involving Italians was discovered by the Austrian Government.

Artifoni invited Joyce to join the Berlitz staff in Trieste. He and Nora moved there on the first Sunday of March 1905. They were to spend most of the next ten years there.

View of the Grand Canal, Trieste. 'In the canal here the boats are lined along the quays.' (*Letters*)

In Joyce's day the beautiful Adriatic port of Trieste was primarily Italian, *Trieste* though it belonged, like Pola, to Austria. Unlike the more provincial Pola, it included a generous mixture of Greeks (Joyce frequented the Orthodox church near the Verdi Theatre, facing the harbour, and compared its ritual unfavourably with that of Rome), Jews (he had begun to identify their exile with his), Turks, Albanians and Slavs. The Archduke Maximilian, who built white Miramare Castle for his wife Charlotte, was not the only Northerner to fall in love with Trieste – Ibsen had seen it as the epitome of the 'beauty of the South' and Rainer Maria Rilke was even in Joyce's day writing the *Duineser Elegien* there, naming them after another castle.

Joyce feared that the 'damn silly sun' of the South 'that turns men to butter' would take the edge from his satirical scorn for Ireland, Irishmen, the Church, priests, betrayers of all kinds. It did, perhaps, thereby helping to mature his Chaucerian view of life and his impersonal acceptance of extremes.

Meanwhile he was unhappy. When it became obvious that Nora was pregnant, the landlady at 3 Piazza Ponterosso asked them to move; luckily Joyce found a more indulgent one at 31 via San Nicolò, next door to the Scuola Berlitz. Artifoni and his assistant turned out to be petty and scheming, his fellow English teacher, a cockney, patronizing. Joyce's continual economic crises bothered him. Worst of all was Nora's petulance owing to her pregnancy and her dissatisfaction with Trieste. Never much of a housewife, she now refused to cook, boggled at going out and wept at slight provocations. These Joyce increased by being frequently drunk in the socialist workers' cafés in the Città Vecchia. Although his teaching was lively, he looked on it as a badly paid grind which was keeping him from his real work. He thought of returning to Dublin and of impractical money-making schemes. He felt that he was on trial and on his silent accusers he pronounced the verdict he had written earlier, sending Stanislaus copies of 'The Holy Office' with instructions for their distribution.

He also sent *Chamber Music* to a London publisher, Grant Richards. Before his son Giorgio was born on 27 July 1905, Joyce had finished twenty-one chapters of the novel and three more *Dubliners* stories – 'A Painful Case', 'The Boarding House' and 'Counterparts'. By the autumn he had completed the dozen stories that he then thought would comprise the book and sent them to Richards (who eventually rejected *Chamber Music*) early in December. In spite of his misgivings about having written a caricature of Dublin life, Joyce felt that the stories were saved by their naturalistic accuracy of detail ('my nicely polished looking-glass') and 'the special odour of corruption' floating over them, making them a 'chapter of moral history' of Ireland that could be 'the first step towards the spiritual liberation of my country'.

This view of his work as moral fable continued throughout Joyce's career in easy co-existence with his view of the artist as amoral, indifferent – like the God of creation paring his finger-nails beyond his handiwork. The one was an inheritance from Dante, Blake, Shelley and D'Annunzio, the other from Aristotle, Aquinas, Flaubert and Oscar Wilde. A part of the 'composite of incompatibilities' which Francini had noticed in Joyce's personality, the seeming contradiction has bothered many critics, who plump for one side or the other. But Joyce, freeing himself from both botherations, makes Stephen

Two views of the Berlitz School in the Piazza Ponterosso, Trieste.

Dedalus in *Ulysses* quote with approval Whitman's well-known catechizing of himself: 'Do I contradict myself? Very well, then, I contradict myself.'

Grant Richards's printer plumped for the moral side. Richards accepted the book and Joyce signed a contract in March. But when Joyce sent 'Two Gallants' to Richards as the thirteenth story, the printer 'descended with his blue pencil full of the Holy Ghost' and objected to its immorality and to that of several other stories as well. Richards called for changes. Joyce – who meanwhile had finished another story, 'A Little Cloud' – argued against making the changes, and Richards in the end refused to publish the book. The battle thus joined over *Dubliners* was to continue, though the opponents shifted, until 1914.

Joyce had finally persuaded Stanislaus to join him in Trieste. The younger *Stanislaus Joyce* brother was only twenty years old and had misgivings, but in October 1905 he agreed to accept an opening at the Scuola Berlitz. The frugal, cautious, abstemious Stanislaus lent Joyce money on his arrival and became, as he later called himself, his 'brother's keeper', playing the ant to Joyce's grasshopper, budgeter to spender, cop to bum, 'straight man' to comedian. Even in appearance the brothers were in striking contrast – Stanislaus sober, short, broadshouldered; Joyce gay, thin, loose-jointed, fragile: Shaun the postman and Shem the penman, as Joyce pictured the two of them in *Finnegans Wake*, like post and pen, stone and stem.

Trieste. The Piazza della Borsa. '*La nostra bella Trieste!* I have often said that angrily but tonight I feel it true.' (*Letters*)

Joyce arranged for Stanislaus to live with him, Nora and Giorgio. They pooled their wages, but these proved inadequate to pay for Joyce's drinking and the daily dining out of the family. He continued to borrow and to collect advances on his pay. When the Francini Brunis, also living in Trieste, proposed that they and the Joyces take a flat together, Joyce was pleased to accept; the two families moved in February to 1 via Giovanni Boccaccio.

In May Artifoni told the Joyce brothers that only one of them could be supported by the school during the slack summer months. Joyce secured a job with a bank in Rome as a foreign correspondence clerk. Late in July 1906, he, Nora and Giorgio left Trieste, leaving Stanislaus behind to serve Berlitz and deal with creditors.

Joyce disliked Rome. It gave him bad dreams of 'death, corpses, assassinations' in which he himself appeared. The hours in the bank were long and he had to write more than two hundred letters a day. Never much impressed by arts other than literature, drama and song, he told Stanislaus that Italian painters had done nothing but 'illustrate a page or two of the New Testament'. He was 'outrageously, illogically sick' of Italy, Italian and Italians. He wrote almost nothing.

He did, however, revise two of the most doubtful stories in *Dubliners*: 'After the Race' and 'A Painful Case', and he conceived a half-dozen stories which were never written. One of these was to be called 'Ulysses' and to deal with a Dublin Jew named Hunter, reputed to be a cuckold. Although he did not get any farther than the title, he kept the character in mind for the time when he could imagine himself cuckolded.

His distaste for Rome helped him think more kindly of Ireland. He wrote to his Aunt Josephine for a map of Dublin, photographs of the country and a book of historical documents. He began to feel that *Dubliners* was 'unnecessarily harsh', not portraying Dublin's hospitality, ingenuous insularity or beauty. His mellower attitude led him to soften 'Grace' and conceive a new story, 'The Dead', of greater dimensions than the others.

Contrasting aspects of Joyce's Dublin: Bull Alley (*left*) and the Bank of Ireland (*right*), across from Trinity College.

By February he was drinking more and spending more. He was depressed and foresaw his 'mental extinction' if he stayed on as a clerk in Rome. Through the good offices of Arthur Symons, Elkin Mathews had agreed to publish *Chamber Music*, and Joyce received proofs in February. But the book no longer pleased him: 'A page of "A Little Cloud" gives me more pleasure than all my verses,' he told Stanislaus, but publishers continued to reject *Dubliners*. He had reached a crisis of disappointment: 'My mouth is full of decayed teeth and my soul of decayed ambitions.' Besides, in spite of their sleeping head to foot as Bloom and Molly sleep in *Ulysses*, Nora was pregnant again. Joyce took his family back to Trieste early in March 1907.

Return to Trieste   Almost seven lean years followed their return, years filled with disappointments and frustrations. Even though he owed him money, Joyce again moved his family in with Francini; then he found rooms at 1 via Santa Catarina. He taught again for 'Herr Berlitz', as he called the Berlitz School. Roberto Prezioso asked him to write some articles on Ireland for *Il Piccolo della Sera*. As Joyce said to Stanislaus, 'I may not be the Jesus Christ I once fondly imagined myself, but I think I must have a talent for journalism.' His talent extended to a series of three public lectures in the spring of 1907 at the Università Popolare. He gained a measure of local acclaim for his writing and lecturing in Italian, which he was now virtually perfect in and which was the language spoken in his home.

Joyce's own work, however, did not progress. Since beginning 'The Dead' in Rome he had written nothing. In April Stanislaus had to dissuade him from telegraphing to Elkin Mathews not to publish *Chamber Music*, which Joyce felt was 'false' and 'feudal' since he had never loved anyone or anything except God.

By July Joyce was so disgruntled that he wrote to the South Africa Colonisation Society for a job. He was prevented from following up his application when he fell ill with rheumatic fever. He spent part of July and August in the city hospital, where late in July he was joined by Nora, who on 26 July gave birth to Lucia Anna in the paupers' ward. Joyce's recovery from the fever was slow, Lucia was a testy child who cried a lot, Giorgio was resentful and demanding, Nora was dissatisfied with the miserable adjoining rooms which they called home, and Stanislaus became in fact his brother's keeper. When Herr Berlitz sold the Trieste school to two of his teachers, Joyce compounded the family's difficulties by resigning his teaching job, though he retained several of his pupils.

But his illness had given Joyce time to reflect and to confirm his resolve patiently to carve the career to which he had been called years before, but which was still largely unformed. In September he finished 'The Dead'. He also

Joyce's sister Eileen, presumably in 1915 when she was married. (The man in this photograph is not her husband.)

Stanislaus Joyce in Trieste. 'My goldfashioned bother near drave me roven mad. . . .' (*Finnegans Wake*)

re-conceived *Stephen Hero* as a five-chapter novel, to be called *A Portrait of the Artist as a Young Man*, and began to re-write it in a new style and a new tone. He had finished the first three chapters by April 1908, and then, discouraged, laid it aside. He revived the idea of 'Ulysses' as a short novel. And he began to see himself as a 'poorjoist' supporting a gay house in a slum of despond.

He had good reason to despond – more rejections of *Dubliners*, an ill-omened attack of iritis, arguments with Nora, too little money. He drank heavily.

Nora, her son Giorgio, and her mother photographed in Galway, 1912.

Stanislaus wrote in his diary for 12 September 1908 that he had saved his brother and his family from starvation six times. To increase his fortune, and in much the same spirit as that in which he had entered a puzzle contest several years before, Joyce formed plans to sell Irish tweeds in Trieste, to seek an appointment in the British Civil Service, to win a scholarship to the Royal University, to pursue a singing career, to apply for a teaching job in Florence.

Partly as an escape from his worries, he attended the theatre a good deal, using Francini's press pass from *Il Piccolo*. He empathized strangely with the action, writhing in pain, making wild gestures, crying out during performances.

Joyce with Giorgio in Trieste.

The empathy was of a piece with the other mimetic elements in the development of his personality – the childhood acting which was Stanislaus's first memory of Joyce, the public appearances with his parents at the Bray Boat Club, the charades at the Sheehys', the 'taking off' of the Rector at Belvedere, the imaging of himself as Parnell, Hamlet, Daedalus, Dante, Byron, Stephen Protomartyr, Lucifer and Jesus. Like his drunkenness and his fainting, the mimesis in life and art forestalled his schizoidal tendencies while enabling him to become Shem the Penman (a 'sham' and Jim the Penman, a famous forger) writing a forged cheque on the world, for he was mimicking his own life as he lived it.

Visits to Dublin It was time for him to return to Dublin to see how that life was getting on. He went with Giorgio in July 1909 for a stay of six weeks. He was welcomed by his sisters and somewhat reconciled with his father, who had resented his elopement. Joyce coolly renewed acquaintance with those who were to people his unfinished books. He was pleased to learn that Mary Sheehy was to marry Thomas Kettle, an MP and the only Dublin reviewer of *Chamber Music*. During the first week of his visit he spent an afternoon with J. F. Byrne at his home at 7 Eccles Street, which became Bloom's house in *Ulysses* and perhaps the best-known address in literature. He also paid renewed attention to Dublin sights and sounds, including those of the offices shared by the *Evening Telegraph* and the *Freeman's Journal*, where Bloom observes the machines:

> Sllt. The nethermost deck of the first machine jogged forward its flyboard with sllt the first batch of quirefolded papers. Sllt. Almost human the way it sllt to call attention. Doing its level best to speak. That door too sllt creaking, asking to be shut. Everything speaks in its own way. Sllt.

Joyce continued his professional journalism by reviewing for *Il Piccolo della Sera* the première at the Abbey Theatre of George Bernard Shaw's *The Shewing-Up of Blanco Posnet*, which had been banned in England.

Abbey Theatre performance of Shaw's *The Shewing-Up of Blanco Posnet* in 1909.

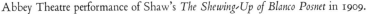
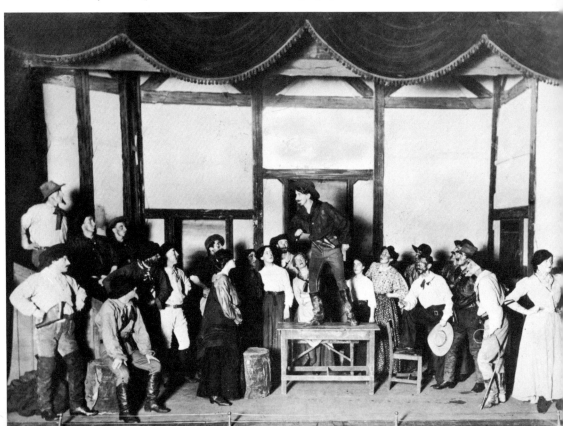

The old Abbey Theatre.
Interior (*below*) and sketches of the audience following performances of Synge's *Playboy of the Western World*, 1907.

7 Eccles Street, the house of Joyce's friend,
J. F. Byrne, and later the address of
Leopold Bloom in *Ulysses*.
Painting by Flora H. Mitchell.

He surveyed the Dublin scene for betrayers, and found Gogarty and Cosgrave. Gogarty, he thought, had sold his soul for material comforts. He visited him at home and, like Monte Cristo refusing muscatel grapes, refused offers of 'grog, wine, coffee, tea'. But he made use of the visit, for the character of Robert Hand in *Exiles* and Buck Mulligan in *Ulysses*. Robert Hand was also made up in part of Cosgrave, the Lynch of the *Portrait*. Joyce also spent time with Cosgrave, drinking and talking, during his visit. Cosgrave, who had failed to secure Nora's favours in 1904, when Joyce had succeeded, now took his revenge by asserting that he had been successful with her.

Cosgrave's claim precipitated a serious crisis in Joyce's life. For just as he carried ambiguously in the pocket of his second-hand trousers the borrowed money to pay for his own betrayal, so, too, Joyce needed and feared cuckoldry.

Having substituted his life in exile with Nora for the authoritarian security of God and the Virgin in the Catholic Church, and having found in their life together a substitute, too, for the family and nation he had abandoned, he had to believe in his new mother-father-church. But, paradoxically, if he could find evidence to destroy his new faith, he could support his commitment to his original apostasy. In tears he wrote immediately to Nora to express his total despair: 'O, Nora, Nora . . . tonight I have learnt that the only thing I believed in was not loyal to me.'

On 7 August he wandered the streets of Dublin dragging the ruins of his life with him. Next day he visited Byrne at 7 Eccles Street, where he 'wept and groaned and gesticulated in futile impotence' as he told him of Cosgrave's allegations. Byrne, knowing his Irishmen, discerned a lying plot by Cosgrave and Gogarty to ruin the Joyce who was casting them badly in his fiction.

Emotionally satisfied by the deviousness of Byrne's analysis, Joyce recovered from his self-pity, or at least sent it on a new tack. He repented his accusation of Nora even before he received a letter from Stanislaus, testifying that in 1904 Cosgrave had confessed to being turned down by Nora in favour of Joyce. Joyce wrote to his 'sweet noble Nora' calling himself 'worthless' and 'contemptible'. He asked her to take him again into her arms so that they could 'defeat this cowardly plot'.

He signed a new contract for the publication of *Dubliners*, with the Dublin firm Maunsel and Company, on more favourable terms than those Grant Richards had given him. Then he and Giorgio visited Nora's home in Galway for a week-end, where Joyce looked eagerly for the image of his loved Nora's girlhood. He wrote her tender letters and bought an expensive gift to give her on his return.

But the fissure caused by this crisis of belief in himself went very deep and revealed sado-masochistic elements which he had not recognized clearly till now. He wrote to Nora:

Tonight I have an idea madder than usual. I feel I would like to be flogged by you. I would like to see your eyes blazing with anger.

I wonder is there some madness in me. Or is love madness? One moment I see you like a virgin or madonna, the next moment I see you shameless, insolent, half-naked and obscene.

The devils would be cast out finally only in his writing – in Chapter Five of the *Portrait*, in *Exiles*, in the Circe episode of *Ulysses*. But he felt that Nora had to become his mother-muse-goddess:

Guide me, my saint, my angel. . . . I will become indeed the poet of my race. I feel this Nora, as I write it. My body soon will penetrate into yours. O that my soul could too! O that I could nestle in your womb like a child born of your flesh and blood, be fed by your blood, sleep in the warm secret gloom of your body!

Looking intently within this self-addressed envelope, we can trace to their biographical roots the motifs of auto-eroticism, incest, sado-masochism and homosexuality in Joyce's writings. In the letter quoted above, Joyce's identity is curiously centred in his penis, which is also at once his child and himself, while Nora is herself and his mother; so that the incest fantasy is twice doubled, then raised to higher powers by the religious and patriotic components. But what do the roots signify in relation to the tree Igdrasil so splendidly flowering above them? That tree is all we know and all we need to know. In his letter to

The Volta Theatre, 45 Mary Street, Dublin, where Joyce opened a 'cinematograph' on 20 December 1909.

Nora, Joyce was acting out his new conception of the *Portrait*, brought to a climax with the scene in which he becomes psychologically his own mother when 'in the virgin womb of the imagination the word was made flesh'.

With the signing of the new *Dubliners* contract Joyce's business in Dublin was finished. His sister Eva accompanied him and Giorgio when they returned to Trieste on 9 September. The new exile was short, though sweet enough because Nora received him as a long-lost lover. Then he saw an opportunity to make his fortune at last by opening a cinema in Dublin, which had none, though cinemas were common enough in Trieste. He quickly persuaded two Triestine entrepreneurs to back the venture and returned to Dublin in October.

He remained there until January 1910, founding the short-lived Volta Theatre, and also achieving an earlier commercial ambition, that of becoming agent in Trieste for Donegal tweeds. His correspondence with Nora, in spite of their brief but loving reunion, remained suspicious, volatile, masochistic, and unusually aggressive against mother Ireland: 'I see nothing on every side of me but the image of the adulterous priest and his servants and of sly deceitful women.' And: 'Are you with me, Nora, or are you secretly against me? I am a jealous, lonely, dissatisfied, proud man.'

Joyce was also, however, an exceedingly romantic man, conceiving of the soul in a way which combined the conceptions of Ignatius Loyola, John Donne, Shelley, Elizabeth Barrett Browning and Gabriele D'Annunzio. He wrote to Nora in what he would later call his 'marmalady' style (and would employ with detachment in the languorous, trembling, swooning passages in Chapter Four of the *Portrait*); he was disappointed at her reaction to *Madama Butterfly* because, he said, 'I wanted to feel your soul swaying with languor and longing as mine did when she sings the romance of her hope. . . .' He visited Finn's Hotel, where Nora had worked when he met her, and wept. Seeing the room Nora had used, he gave up for once his role as Jesus. He assigned it to Nora, while he became, humbly if somewhat hysterically, the Three Wise Men from the East praying at the bed-altar-manger:

Yes, I too have felt at moments the burning in my soul of that pure fire which burns for ever on the altar of my love's heart. I could have knelt by that little bed and abandoned myself to a flood of tears. The tears were besieging my eyes as I stood looking at it. I could have knelt and prayed there as the three kings from the East knelt and prayed before the manger in which Jesus lay. They had travelled over deserts and seas and brought their gifts and wisdom and royal trains to kneel before a little new-born child and I had brought my errors and follies and sins and wondering and longing to lay them at the little bed in which a young girl had dreamed of me.

When Joyce took his follies back to Trieste in January 1910, another sister, Eileen, followed in his train. He returned to the humdrum of his lessons. The Volta failed. George Roberts and his printer had second thoughts about *Dubliners* and asked for changes. His creditors continued their demands, Stanislaus grumbled. They moved again, to 32 via Barriera Vecchia, where in a fit of depression and bafflement Joyce threw the unfinished manuscript of the *Portrait* into the fire. Although Eileen rescued it, Joyce did not have the heart to work on it and it was stored away.

Instead of turning life into art, he reversed the process and half-engineered a relationship sometime in 1911 between Nora and Prezioso, the effeminate editor of *Il Piccolo della Sera*. Nora reported the moves of Prezioso's suit, much as Bertha reports to Richard in *Exiles*, and Joyce accepted them as grist for his mill. But Joyce stopped the mill when the potential adultery seemed likely to become actual. He forgot the principles of his fictional exile, and the quiet and compassionate acceptance of a similar prospect by Bloom, and confronted Prezioso in the name of friendship. Contrite, Prezioso wept.

The year 1912, Joyce's thirtieth, was the most disheartening of his life. His domestic arrangements remained precarious, and the annoying objections of George Roberts and his printer to *Dubliners* – among them to Joyce's use of the real names of public houses in certain stories – continued, preventing him from completing the *Portrait*, which had been tied up in an old sheet after Eileen had saved it from the flames. While Joyce's career as a writer had hardly begun, he continued his side lines as language teacher, public lecturer, journalist and tweed salesman.

He decided to return to Dublin, this time with Nora and the children, to try to persuade Roberts to fulfil his contract and publish *Dubliners*. In July the family travelled to Galway, where Joyce and Nora paid a sentimental visit to the cemetery where the Michael Furey of 'The Dead' is buried. In Dublin, Joyce failed to persuade Roberts to publish, even though he agreed to make a few changes in the text and to leave out 'An Encounter'. But though the sheets were already printed, Roberts and the printer had them destroyed on 11 September. Joyce and his family started back to Trieste that night, lest 'the old sow that eats her farrow' should finally have her meal of them.

On the way back, Joyce wrote his last broadside pasquinade, 'Gas from a Burner', in which he pictured George Roberts, a former traveller in ladies' underwear, defending his courage as a publisher:

> *I printed folklore from North and South*
> *By Gregory of the Golden Mouth:*
> *I printed poets, sad silly and solemn:*

I printed Patrick What-do-you-Colm:
I printed the great John Millicent Synge
Who soars above on an angel's wing
In the playboy shift that he pinched as swag
From Maunsel's manager's travelling-bag.

*   *   *

Shite and onions! Do you think I'll print
The name of the Wellington Monument,
Sydney Parade and Sandymount tram,
Downes's cakeshop and Williams's jam?

Joyce had the broadside printed in Trieste on his arrival and sent it back to his brother Charles for distribution as his parting shot at a Dublin which he would never visit again except in his books.

J. M. Synge, 1907.

Wellington Monument.

I. Downes's cakeshop.

"I Don't Care a Rap."

In 1913 Joyce's fortunes turned. He found a better job teaching English in the Scuola Superiore di Commercio Revoltella. This, in turn, brought him more private pupils. Stanislaus found them a better flat at 4 via Donato Bramante, only two doors from the Piazza Giambattista Vico. His proximity to this monument to the philosopher whose *Scienza Nuova* became a shaping influence on *Ulysses* and *Finnegans Wake* must have seemed prophetic to Joyce, always on the lookout for signs of his destiny; perhaps it recalled too his first brief teaching job on Vico Road, Dalkey. He discussed Vico frequently with one of his Triestine students, for his teaching method was to talk with a pupil about whatever interested both of them.

He and his pupil Amalia Popper, daughter of a Jewish businessman named Leopoldo, became interested in one another. For about a year Joyce taught her and loved her with a sudden resurgence of his youthful idealism – a love which he recorded romantically in several of the poems which were to become part of *Pomes Penyeach* ('A Flower Given to My Daughter', 'Watching the Needle-boats at San Sabba', 'Nightpiece' and 'Tutto e Sciolto'), and ironically in a notebook called *Giacomo Joyce* to parody his own romantic passion by comparing it to the philandering of Giacomo Casanova. Amalia also became a good part of the shadowy Emma in the last chapter of the *Portrait* and something of Molly Bloom in *Ulysses*. There, too, he would have his emotion both ways in a satisfying ambivalence.

Once a few things had begun to look up, many others did. At the end of November, Grant Richards asked to see *Dubliners* again. In December Ezra *Ezra Pound* Pound, who had heard of Joyce from Yeats, wrote to ask if Joyce had anything he wanted published in one of the several magazines with which Pound had influence. Before Joyce replied, the 'factive' Pound wrote again to say that he would pay to use 'I hear an army charging upon the land' in his *Des Imagistes* anthology. In January 1914, Joyce sent him this poem, Chapter One of the *Portrait* and a copy of *Dubliners*. Within a week Pound replied that the *Portrait*

Piazza Giambattista Vico, Trieste.
'Old Vico Roundpoint.' (*Finnegans Wake*)

Ezra Pound, 1916.

was first rate – he compared Joyce's prose to that of James, Conrad and Hudson – and that he was sending the chapter to Dora Marsden, editor of *The Egoist*. A

few days later he wrote praising *Dubliners* and saying that he was sending 'An Encounter', 'The Boarding House', and 'A Little Cloud' to H. L. Mencken, editor of *Smart Set*. The generous Pound had discovered Joyce as surely as he had discovered Yeats and was soon to discover Eliot, though to them and many others he would act more as teacher and less as a literary agent.

But as a literary agent Pound was superb. Miss Marsden immediately agreed to publish the *Portrait* as a serial beginning in the issue of 2 February – a date of good omen, Joyce felt, for it was his birthday. Mencken, too, took Pound's bait. Joyce was so encouraged that he wrote to Richards demanding a decision on *Dubliners*. On 29 January Richards agreed to publish and the book came out on 15 June 1914, the eve of the tenth anniversary of the 'Bloomsday' taking shape in Joyce's mind.

Joyce had still to write the last two chapters of the *Portrait*, which he had not worked on since 1908. His last two visits to Dublin and the episode with Amalia Popper had clarified for him some of the themes and tones of these magnificent chapters. Early in November he wrote the final lines of Stephen's diary, memorized since by many a schoolboy:

Welcome, O life! I go to encounter for the millionth time the reality of experience. . . . Old father, old artificer, stand me now and ever in good stead.

As he put it in *Finnegans Wake*, 'His jymes is out of a job, would sit and write.' So Joyce set to work on *Exiles*, the play for which he had begun making notes a year before, and on the first episodes of *Ulysses*, which had been on his mind for a decade. But their completion had to wait on the fortunes of the war which had begun in July between Austria and Serbia.

For Stanislaus, who was well known in Trieste for his pro-Italian and anti-clerical opinions, the war meant internment by the Austrian Government in January 1915. For Joyce, less political and more subtle in his outspokenness, it meant going to another exile in neutral Zürich the following June. Confident that his star was rising, pushed by Pound and his friends in England and the United States, Joyce was at first impressed by the *bürgerliche* cleanliness of the city, which he contrasted with the 'dear dirt' of Dublin and the easy-going chaos of Trieste.

Although he soon found a few pupils, he had no other employment except for his writing, and no money. But through the persistent generosity of relatives, friends and unknown admirers he began a new way of financing his career by means of gifts. At first these included regular remittances from Nora's uncle,

Michael Healy,
Nora's uncle.

Michael Healy, and grants from such bodies as the British Royal Literary Fund, the Civil List and the Society of Authors – all instigated by Yeats at the urging of Pound.

Joyce's contract with Richards for *Dubliners* provided that royalties be paid after 500 copies were sold, but the 1914 sales stood at 499 copies. In 1915 the sales dwindled to a few dozen, and in 1916 to fewer still. Disheartening too, after his nine-year battle over the publication of *Dubliners*, was the disinclination of publishers to bring out the *Portrait*. In 1915 five publishers declined the book. Miss Harriet Shaw Weaver, who had taken over the editorship of *The Egoist* from Miss Marsden, offered to publish it herself and Joyce agreed, after which seven printers refused to set the type. One of the most respected publisher's readers, Edward Garnett, thought the book 'too discursive, formless, unrestrained', and suggested that it needed a complete re-writing to 'shape it more carefully as the product of the craftsmanship, mind and imagination of an artist.'

James Joyce (*left*), about 1915.

Harriet Shaw Weaver,
Joyce's patron; *A Portrait of the Artist
as a Young Man* was first serialized
in her magazine, *The Egoist*.

Meanwhile, in New York B. W. Huebsch, a novice publisher who had been
struck in 1914 by the excellence of *Dubliners*, read the *Portrait* in June 1916 and
wrote to Miss Weaver offering to publish it. In spite of Joyce's difficulties in
getting the book between covers, it had already proved more profitable to him
than either *Chamber Music* or *Dubliners*. Miss Weaver, presaging generosity to
come, had paid him £25 for serializing it in *The Egoist* and had advanced
another £25 when she agreed to publish it in book form. Huebsch, too, gave
him a £54 advance on royalties.

73 Seefeldstrasse, Zürich. Joyce lived in Apartment 3 from January to October 1917. 'I stopped here as it is the first big city after the frontier.' (*Letters*)

Café Terrasse, Zürich, in 1915 (*right*).

Zürich   In Zürich Joyce made friends rapidly, partly through his frequent changes of residence, partly through the cafés he went to, where his gaiety and infectious laughter and his Dubliner's talent as wit, raconteur and drinker made him popular. The family stayed briefly at the Gasthaus Hoffnung, where Joyce and Nora had honeymooned eleven years before. Within a few months they had lived at 7 Reinhardstrasse and at 10 Kreuzstrasse; at 54 Seefeldstrasse they remained until 1917, when they moved to 73 Seefeldstrasse. While Joyce had always frequented cafés, they tended, in Pola and Trieste, to be the cheaper sort used by sailors and working-men. In Zürich, however, he chose first-class cafés and restaurants, as if he had just won a school prize. These included the Restaurant zum Roten Kreuz, the Café Terrasse, the Café Voltaire (frequented by early Surrealists like Tristan Tzara and Hans Arp) and the Café Odéon,

Café Odéon, Zürich: interior *right*, exterior *opposite*.

Pfauen Hotel and Restaurant, Zürich. '. . . I should like a litre of Fendant in that famous corner.' (*Letters*)

Stefan Zweig.   Frank Wedekind.   Romain Rolland.

The Joyce family, Zürich, 1915. 'I am here with wife and children (two aged ten and eight).' (*Letters*)

where Joyce may have met Lenin, a steady customer. His regular café for the war years, however, was the more comfortable and less high-toned Pfauen Café, where his friends have recalled him seated with a bottle of one of his favourite white wines 'exchecking strong verbs' with other regulars. The wine most often associated with Joyce is the Swiss Fendant de Sion, though he enjoyed many of the white wines, including Neufchâtel, Riesling and even white Chianti.

The pleasant shores of the Zürichsee, protected by the surrounding mountains, attracted many war refugees. There were so many from south-eastern Europe that the Swiss nicknamed the Bahnhofstrasse the 'Balkanstrasse'. Joyce's temperament made him partial to Jews and Greeks, but he also enjoyed the acquaintance of well-known writers – Frank Wedekind, Romain Rolland, René Schickele and Stefan Zweig. Many of the refugees were professional playwrights, actors and directors who made Zürich for a time the centre of the modern theatre movement begun by Ibsen.

Great conductors came, too, and there were many international exhibitions of painting – but painting was an art to which Joyce responded only in literary terms. In music his interest lay in songs with words, and in painting he liked portraits and pictures which told a story: if he thought the story needed to be made more explicit, he would label the picture. Later in Paris he had the chance to 'dictate' a drawing of himself done by César Abin, and demanded an elaborate cartoon full of meanings. He had little taste in furnishings or architecture ('no taste – only genius,' as one friend said). His main concession to more abstract arts was the expressive dancing which he often performed during evening drinking-bouts. Even *Finnegans Wake*, though musical, stuffs its portmanteau words with meaning upon meaning.

Patrons Although Joyce now had a growing international reputation as a writer, he remained intermittently in financial straits until 1917, when an anonymous admirer began sending him £50 every three months through a London solicitor. The gift, neither the last nor the largest from Harriet Shaw Weaver, enabled Joyce to concentrate on writing *Ulysses*. It also helped him to bear with some equanimity the onslaught of glaucoma and other diseases of the retina which, though operable, tended to lead to blindness in those days.

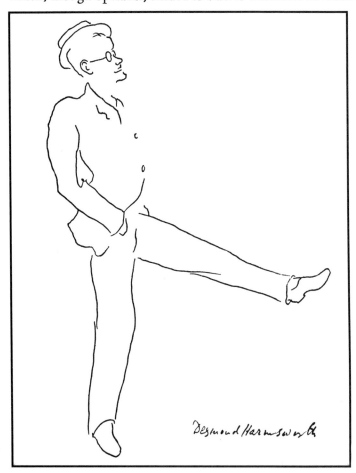

Joyce's Dance, by Desmond Harmsworth.

Caricature of Joyce ▶ by César Abin.

Cesar ABIN

Because of his relative affluence, Joyce decided to spend the winter of 1917–18 in Locarno, a beautiful resort on the south side of the Alps in Italian Switzerland. His doctors thought his eyes might improve in the equable climate, and there he thought Nora, grown nervous and restive from the heavy, wet air of Zürich, might become calm. But late in August Joyce suffered a severe attack of glaucoma which required the first of many operations on his right eye. Nevertheless, in October the family entrained for Locarno.

They settled in the Pension Daheim, just off an agreeable green not far from the Piazza Grande. Joyce put the finishing touches to the first three episodes of *Ulysses* and sent them back to Zürich, where a new friend, Claud Sykes, an American actor, had agreed to type them. The weather was nice enough, but there was no opera, no drama, no friends, and only inferior restaurants. They returned to Zürich in January.

Locarno. 'I am here by doctor's advice and hope the dry air will do me good after my rather bad breakdown.' (*Letters*)

Pension Daheim, Locarno, where Joyce lived from November 1917 to January 1918.

38 Universitätsstrasse, where Joyce lived from January to October 1918.

Pound continued to act for Joyce, encouraging Miss Weaver to publish *Ulysses* as a serial in *The Egoist* and sending the first three episodes to New York to *The Little Review*, run by Margaret Anderson and Jane Heap. When they had read to the sentence 'Signature of all things . . .' Miss Anderson said, 'We'll print it if it's the last effort of our lives.' And so they did, beginning in March 1918, and so it almost was. The American censors organized against the book much as the Irish and English censors had against *Dubliners* and the *Portrait*.

Before the censors descended, however, another good thing and another interesting thing happened to Joyce. The good thing was that Zürich's richest expatriate and fashionable analysand, Mrs Harold McCormick, only daughter of John D. Rockefeller, Sr, began to pay Joyce 1,000 Swiss francs a month, a sum which brought his monthly income up to nearly £60 (about $300). He dropped some of his English students and spent more time at the Pfauen Café when he was not writing *Ulysses*, at another flat part way up the hill at 38 Universitätsstrasse.

The interesting thing might be called 'The Affair of Henry Carr's Trousers'. It began because Joyce was persuaded by Claud Sykes that the two of them could serve Allied cultural propaganda and make money to boot if they organized an acting company. The company called itself The English Players and was to open with Oscar Wilde's *The Importance of Being Earnest*. Among the amateur actors signed up at ten francs a performance was Henry Carr, a minor official of the British Consulate, who having agreed to play Algernon went out and bought himself a pair of trousers, a hat and a pair of gloves for the role.

The play was performed before an enthusiastic audience on the evening of 29 April 1918 at the Theater zur Kaufleuten on Pelikanstrasse. Partners Sykes and Joyce were assured of a profit. But when Joyce handed Carr the ten francs agreed upon Carr was annoyed: he had spent 150 francs on his new trousers and the rest of his outfit.

Joyce was angry in his turn. He accosted Carr in the Consulate and, in the presence of two other employees, demanded from Carr the money for the tickets he had sold. Carr brought up the trousers. Joyce brought up Carr's patriotism. Carr burst out: 'You're a cad. . . . You're a swindler. If you don't get out, I'll throw you down the stairs.' Joyce objected that Carr's language was not fit for a government office. He wrote to the Consul-General, A. Percy Bennett, asking him to dismiss Carr, and to the Zürich police asking them for protection. The Consul-General supported Carr and withdrew the official support he had given to the Players. On 3 May Joyce sued Carr for libel and the twenty-five francs he alleged Carr owed him for tickets. He also took his case, by correspondence, to the top and wrote to Sir Horace Rumbold, the British Minister in Berne.

Café Zimmerleuten, Zürich, about 1917.

Portrait of Joyce
by Frank Budgen.

While the case dragged on, Joyce spent the days working on *Ulysses* and the nights drinking – usually with Frank Budgen, an English painter, and August Suter, a Swiss sculptor, both of whom had come to Zürich from Paris at the beginning of the war. They became Joyce's close friends. One of their parties at the Zimmerleuten went on until dawn, Joyce having invited the owner, cooks, waiters and chambermaids to drink with them after the place closed. When he was drunk he used to enjoy singing and dancing and reciting poetry in several languages. Nora usually stayed at home with the children. But in the cafés, as Budgen put it in *James Joyce and the Making of 'Ulysses'*:

He was always looking and listening for the necessary fact or word. . . . And as, in a sense, the theme of *Ulysses* is the whole of life, there was no end to the variety of material that went into its building. . . . I have seen him collect in the space of a few hours the oddest assortment of material: a parody on the

Programme of The English Players'
first production at the Pfauen
Theater in Zürich.

House that Jack Built, the name and action of a poison, the method of caning boys on training ships, the wobbly cessation of a tired unfinished sentence, the nervous trick of a convive turning his glass in inward-turning circles, a Swiss music-hall joke turning on a pun in Swiss dialect, . . .

His progress on *Ulysses* was swift, and *The Little Review* continued to publish the episodes as he sent them through Pound. Joyce's reputation grew with each episode and with the favourable reviews of *Exiles*, published but not yet produced as a play.

Although Joyce planned that The English Players should produce it, they did not do so. Instead, they arranged a triple bill of one-act plays – Barrie's *The Twelve-Pound Look*, Synge's *Riders to the Sea* and Shaw's *The Dark Lady of the Sonnets* – which they presented on 17 June 1918 at the Pfauen Theater, an elegant scarlet-plush-and-taffeta house behind the café. It was another triumph –

Photograph of Joyce taken
in Zürich about 1918.

especially Synge's play with Nora in the role of Cathleen and the other players imitating her Galway accent.

Just before the performance Sykes and Joyce received letters from the Consul-General, Bennett, demanding that they volunteer for military duty, though Bennett knew about Joyce's poor eyesight and his neutrality pledge to the Austrian authorities. Joyce was so incensed that he switched to a pro-German newspaper. But he won his case against Carr, and was awarded court costs and sixty francs indemnity, and Carr's countersuit for the cost of his trousers was disallowed. Joyce tasted his revenge for a long time afterwards, and made it complete by transferring all his Zürich consular enemies to the Dublin Inferno of *Ulysses*. Rumbold becomes the Master Barber who writes to the Lord Mayor to apply for the job of hangman in a 'painful case', Private Carr is one of the drunken cads who knock Stephen down in the Circe episode, and Consul-General Bennett his sergeant-major. But the Affair of the Trousers was only one of a thousand events which Joyce fused into the vast book of himself which he kept writing.

As peace settled over Joyce and Europe, his last association with the Players saw him in the unaccustomed position of donor. He received a gift of $1,000 from two Americans, Scofield Thayer and J.S. Watson, Jr, who had been told of his financial troubles by Padraic and Mary Colum, to whom Joyce had advertised them. As he had just been endowed again by Miss Weaver – this time with £5,000 in war bonds at five per cent interest – he felt affluent enough to turn over most of the $1,000 to the Players.

On 9 December, Joyce experienced one of those coincidences which affected him profoundly at the time and which later became material for his books. Walking home up Universitätsstrasse, he saw ahead of him a pretty young woman with a slight limp. For him she was a reincarnation of the girl who, wading in the tidal stream of Dublin Bay two decades before, had converted him to 'mortal beauty'. The young woman was Martha Fleischmann, who was kept by an engineer called Rudolf Hiltpold in a flat at 6 Culman-strasse, only a few blocks from where Joyce lived. Like the wading girl, 'when she felt his presence and the worship of his eyes her eyes turned to him in quiet sufferance of his gaze, without shame or wantonness.' He wrote her love-letters comparing her to the Blessed Virgin and using Greek *e*'s in his signature as Bloom does in his letters to Martha Clifford. Like Bloom's affair with Martha and his *voyeurism* with Gerty McDowell, Joyce's with his Martha was compounded of late-blossoming desire and his passion for watching girls which he parodied in Lenehan the Looker as well as in Bloom and H.C. Earwicker. Among the gifts from his youth which Joyce sent Martha was a copy of *Chamber Music*. When Hiltpold was away, she allowed Joyce to see her, granting him a ritualistic meeting in 1919 on the night of Candlemas (which was also Joyce's birthday). He took her to Budgen's studio and, like a timid Tarquin, tenderly observed his lazy Lucrece by the light of a Chanukah candle placed in a ceremonial candlestick which he had borrowed from one of his former students. As 'Jaysus James', he was pleased to think that his Blessed Virgin was Jewish. This stagey evening was their last meeting.

Meanwhile, Joyce was beginning to think of going back to Trieste, his second home, where Stanislaus and Eileen, with her husband Frantisek Schaurek, and their two children whom Joyce had not seen, had already returned after the Armistice. In August *Exiles* had been performed at Munich and proved, as Joyce said, 'a flop'. He was disturbed, too, by the objections made by Pound and others (even the gentle Miss Weaver) to the Sirens episode of *Ulysses*. And when he called at the bank for his October allowance from Mrs McCormick, he was told that his credit had been cut off.

Martha Fleischmann

Ettore Schmitz (Italo Svevo)
and his family.

It was in the midst of these troubles that Joyce and his family returned in October 1919 to Trieste. There things got worse. Trieste and everyone in it, including Joyce, had changed. No longer the busy port of the 'ramshackle' empire which Joyce had learned to enjoy, Trieste was now a dull provincial city of the Italian kingdom. Stanislaus had gained a new independence in the internment camp and had found friends of his own on his return. He resented the intrusion of his brother's family into the Schaurek flat, where he lived with his sister's family. He bore a few old grudges as well, and he was bored with *Ulysses*. Joyce renewed his friendships with Francini Bruni, Ettore Schmitz and others, but they were not the same either. He took up his old job at the Scuola Superiore di Commercio Revoltella (now the Università di Trieste), but his heart was no longer in it. He lacked energy and told Budgen: 'For six weeks after my arrival I never read nor wrote nor spoke.' He neglected to attend the opera. He even thought briefly of abandoning *Ulysses*, partly because he did not have Budgen to discuss it with. And he had to drink white Chianti instead of Fendant.

But he did get back to work. He finished the Nausicaa episode by his thirty-eighth birthday. Miss Weaver's comments on it pleased him very much. She wrote: '. . . though you are neither priest nor doctor of medicine, I think you have something of both – the Reverend James Joyce, S.J., M.D.' He plunged into the Oxen of the Sun episode, long and difficult to write because the nine stages of the development of Mrs Purefoy's baby in her womb are presented in nine stages of the development of English prose style.

By May he had begun to think of leaving Trieste for the centre of things. Pound had written to him proposing that they meet that summer. Joyce replied with a long letter of complaint about his lack of money and effects – the Italian inflation, the fall in the exchange rate of the English pound, the inadequacy of his wardrobe. This final grievance was dealt with by Pound when Joyce and Giorgio visited him in Sirmione on Lake Garda: he fitted out Joyce with a second-hand suit, a pair of shoes, and the resolve to leave Trieste for London.

Pound's report to John Quinn on Joyce's character was perceptive:

Joyce – pleasing; after the first shell of cantankerous Irishman, I got the impression that the real man is the author of *Chamber Music*, the sensitive. The rest is genius; the registration of realities on the temperament, the delicate temperament of the early poems. A concentration and absorption passing Yeats' – Yeats has never taken on anything requiring the condensation of *Ulysses*.

Paris   In July 1920, the Joyce family said good-bye to their Triestine relatives and friends and headed for London by way of Venice, Milan, Dijon and Paris. They had planned to stop in Paris for only a week or so before going on to settle in London, to be nearer Dublin and Joyce's father. But they remained in Paris for the next twenty years. The departure from Trieste marked the end of Joyce's close relations with Stanislaus, Eileen and his other relatives in Italy, and even those in Ireland; he did not see his father again.

The main reason for Joyce's settling in Paris was that Ezra Pound had prepared the way for him there, putting copies of the *Portrait* into influential hands with plugs such as, 'There's nothing in the literature of the world today, and not much in the literature of the past, that's up to it.' Pound also arranged many introductions for the shy but calculating lion in the thick eyeglasses, second-hand suit and 'leaky sneakers'.

In those days, Paris was the hub and the spokes of the literary universe, perhaps because it was, as Joyce said, 'the last of the human cities'. Pound ran up and down the spokes eagerly. Joyce, from shyness, lack of interest in 'the arts' and dedication to completing the Circe episode by Christmas 1920, sat at

Joyce and Sylvia Beach in the doorway of her bookshop, Shakespeare and Company, Paris, 1920. ▶

Paris, July 1928

18 Rue D'Odéon
Festival of St. James

Cartoon of Joyce and his friends, by F. Scott Fitzgerald, 1928.

Sylvia Beach

the centre of the hub when he was not writing or drinking. The centre was the rue Dupuytren and, round the corner, the rue de l'Odéon, with its two book-shops, Shakespeare and Company, run by Sylvia Beach, a young American from Princeton, New Jersey, and La Maison des Amis des Livres, run by Adrienne Monnier, friend of André Gide, Paul Valéry, Paul Claudel and many other French writers. Joyce met both women on 11 July. A friendship grew up almost immediately between him and Miss Beach, one that was to prove as valuable in its way as that between Joyce and Miss Weaver, for Miss Beach became the publisher of *Ulysses* and *Pomes Penyeach*. She was attracted by his air of quiet dedication – and by the gentleman's cane he carried, the boyish tennis shoes worn with the dark blue serge suit and the black felt hat. She gave Joyce her immediate sympathy, admiration and understanding, provided him with books and attended to the practical details of his life. Through her and through Pound, Joyce met T. S. Eliot, Wyndham Lewis, Valery Larbaud, Marcel Proust, Robert McAlmon, Ernest Hemingway, Sherwood Anderson, Myron and Helen Nutting, Gertrude Stein, Edmond Jaloux, F. Scott Fitz-gerald, Max Eastman, Frank O'Connor and many others.

'The Duc de Joyeux Sings', a lampoon on Joyce by Wyndham Lewis.

Joyce's daughter, Lucia, as a child and as a young woman.

Joyce's Children   Giorgio, now fifteen, and Lucia, also in her teens, were reaching the crises of their adolescence. They had had more than their share of troubles: being brought up as aliens in several different countries, with the attendant confusion of tongues, the interrupted education and feelings of homelessness; moving constantly from one address to another; having for a father a man dedicated to writing unprofitable, difficult books, while artfully dodging bill-collectors and seeking release in daily conviviality and frequent drunkenness. Moreover, Joyce had made 'mistakes' in rearing his children, giving them an undesired freedom from discipline except of an explosive kind. Their identities had to grow around their father's genius, which was of an unusually diverse and complex type, essentially dissociative or centrifugal, held together by continual 'mapmaking' acts of the will. The lives of the children reflect some of the pathos of Joyce's life, a pathos which he understood rather thoroughly but from which he had constantly to protect himself by means of his humour and his writing.

But the heroic element in Joyce's struggle tended to curse the development of the children. By 1920 Lucia's schizophrenia was becoming apparent. It would

The Joyce family in Paris, early 1920s. ▶

Ford Madox Ford, Joyce, Ezra Pound and John Quinn in Pound's Paris studio, 1923.

grow – in many ways a twisted mirror image of Joyce's own dissociative tendencies – in spite of the attention which was given to its cure. And Giorgio,
about to finish his haphazard schooling at the age of sixteen, saw little in the
way of a career open to him. Both he and Lucia made more or less futile efforts
to imitate their father, Giorgio as a singer who got as far as the new National
Broadcasting Corporation in the United States, Lucia as a creative artist
trying first singing, then dancing, writing, and finally the design of delicately
illuminated letters for books. These attempts did not succeed and sorrow became the lot of children and parents alike. Joyce transformed it into the geniality

Joyce in the 1920s.

and reconciliation of *Finnegans Wake*, but pain, nevertheless, lies close beneath the baroquely riffled and elaborated ambivalence of that 'umoroso' book.

First, however, he had to finish *Ulysses*. It had already made him famous through the gradually widening circles of scandal caused by its serial publication in *The Little Review*. It was destined to become a cause as well as a great book. The New York Society for the Prevention of Vice had had copies of *The Little Review* seized, and Miss Anderson and Miss Heap were brought into court in February 1921, and were convicted. Jane Heap's comment that 'no American with an I.Q. over ten was ever tried by a jury of his peers' suggests the attitude

'Ulysses'

of the large number of New York intellectuals and bohemians who filled the courtroom.

One important result of the conviction was that B. W. Huebsch, who had published the *Portrait*, wrote to Joyce in March saying that he could not publish *Ulysses* without some changes in the text. As soon as Joyce told Miss Beach of Huebsch's decision, she suggested that he 'let Shakespeare and Company have the honor of bringing out . . . *Ulysses*'. When Joyce agreed, she made plans for an edition of 1,000 copies to be subscribed in advance, and printed by Darantière of Dijon; Joyce was to receive two-thirds of the net profits. Miss Weaver offered to bring out an English edition with sheets imported from Dijon, and she sent him a £200 advance against royalties.

Joyce had become a legend because of his travels, the gossip of national and international sets in Zürich and Paris, Pound's and Miss Beach's propaganda, the New York trial of *The Little Review*, and the advertised publication of *Ulysses*. As he wrote to Miss Weaver, it was rumoured that he was an espionage agent, a film magnate, a cocaine-sniffer, a mystic and a madman. 'The truth is,' he added, 'that I am a quite commonplace person undeserving of so much imaginative painting', although he acknowledged 'some truth' in the opinion that he was 'a crafty simulating and dissimulating Ulysses-type, a "jejune Jesuit", selfish and cynical.' He also spoke of his 'emptiness':

I have not read a work of literature for several years. My head is full of pebbles and rubbish and broken matches and lots of glass. . . . The task I set myself technically in writing a book from eighteen different points of view and in as many styles all apparently unknown or undiscovered by my fellow tradesmen, that and the nature of the legend chosen would be enough to upset anyone's mental balance.

To a certain extent, Joyce sponsored the legend, just as he preferred that some parts of *Ulysses* remain enigmatic 'to keep the professors busy for centuries. . . .'

By June 1921, Joyce was reading the galley-proofs, adding to them freely in what had become his 'elaborative' manner, and re-writing whole passages throughout the summer and early autumn, while he continued to work on the manuscript. In spite of very severe attacks of iritis and several dead faints from superstitious fear and exhaustion, he completed the Penelope and Ithaca episodes in October. 'Penelope' ended with Molly Bloom's now famous affirmation of life:

and first I put my arms around him yes and drew him down so he could feel my breasts all perfume yes and his heart was going like mad and yes I said yes I will yes.

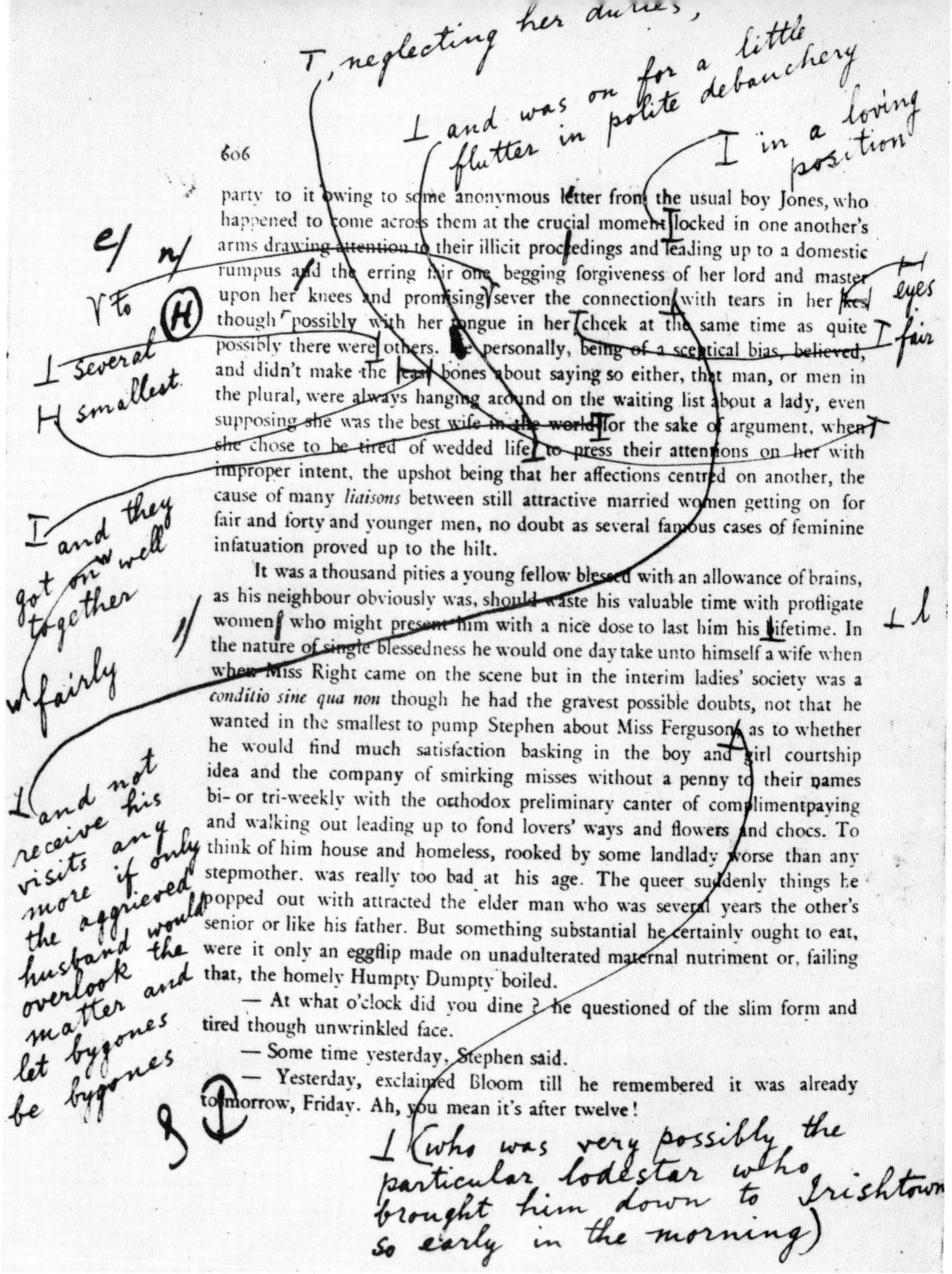

Handwritten annotations (Joyce's corrections):

T, neglecting her duties,

L and was on for a little / flutter in polite debauchery

I in a loving / position

606

party to it owing to some anonymous letter from the usual boy Jones, who
happened to come across them at the crucial moment locked in one another's
arms drawing attention to their illicit proceedings and leading up to a domestic
rumpus and the erring fair one begging forgiveness of her lord and master
upon her knees and promising sever the connection with tears in her eyes
though possibly with her tongue in her cheek at the same time as quite
possibly there were others. He personally, being of a sceptical bias, believed,
and didn't make the least bones about saying so either, that man, or men in
the plural, were always hanging around on the waiting list about a lady, even
supposing she was the best wife in the world for the sake of argument, when
she chose to be tired of wedded life to press their attentions on her with
improper intent, the upshot being that her affections centred on another, the
cause of many *liaisons* between still attractive married women getting on for
fair and forty and younger men, no doubt as several famous cases of feminine
infatuation proved up to the hilt.

It was a thousand pities a young fellow blessed with an allowance of brains,
as his neighbour obviously was, should waste his valuable time with profligate
women who might present him with a nice dose to last him his lifetime. In
the nature of single blessedness he would one day take unto himself a wife when
when Miss Right came on the scene but in the interim ladies' society was a
conditio sine qua non though he had the gravest possible doubts, not that he
wanted in the smallest to pump Stephen about Miss Ferguson as to whether
he would find much satisfaction basking in the boy and girl courtship
idea and the company of smirking misses without a penny to their names
bi- or tri-weekly with the orthodox preliminary canter of complimentpaying
and walking out leading up to fond lovers' ways and flowers and chocs. To
think of him house and homeless, rooked by some landlady worse than any
stepmother. was really too bad at his age. The queer suddenly things he
popped out with attracted the elder man who was several years the other's
senior or like his father. But something substantial he certainly ought to eat,
were it only an eggflip made on unadulterated maternal nutriment or, failing
that, the homely Humpty Dumpty boiled.

— At what o'clock did you dine ? he questioned of the slim form and
tired though unwrinkled face.

— Some time yesterday, Stephen said.

— Yesterday, exclaimed Bloom till he remembered it was already
tomorrow, Friday. Ah, you mean it's after twelve !

(Left margin handwritten):

e/ n/
√ to
(H)

⊥ several smallest.

⊥ and they got on well together fairly

⊥ and not receive his visits any more if only the aggrieved husband would overlook the matter and let bygones be bygones

(Right margin handwritten):

⊥ t

⊥ eyes

⊥ fair

⊥ l

(Bottom handwritten):

⊥ (who was very possibly the particular lodestar who brought him down to Irishtown so early in the morning)

Page proof of *Ulysses*, with Joyce's corrections.

107

Joyce himself had explained the intricate relation of part to part within the book in the 'scheme' (later published by Stuart Gilbert in *James Joyce's 'Ulysses'*) he sent to Carlo Linati in September:

> I have given only catchwords in my scheme but I think you will understand it all the same. It is an epic of two races (Israelite–Irish) and at the same time the cycle of the human body as well as a little story of a day (life). The character of Ulysses always fascinated me – even when a boy. Imagine, fifteen years ago I started writing it as a short story for *Dubliners*! For seven years I have been working at this book – blast it! It is also a sort of encyclopedia. My intention is to transpose the myth *sub specie temporis nostri*. Each adventure (that is, every hour, every organ, every art being interconnected and interrelated in the structural scheme of the whole) should not only condition but even create its own technique. Each adventure is so to say one person although it is composed of persons – as Aquinas relates of the angelic hosts.

Joyce's archaeological-historical-anthropological-psychological novel was, in other words, an attempt to write a book in which all of man's experience was focused in a single day in Dublin – the most concerted effort ever made in the novel to relate every part to every other part and to the whole, often in many ways. It is the most 'conscious' book ever written or, to put it in Aristotelian terms, if 'beauty depends on magnitude and order', then it is the most beautiful book ever written.

At Joyce's insistence and to his great superstitious pleasure, the first three copies of *Ulysses* in their Grecian blue paper binding with white lettering reached Paris on 2 February 1922, his fortieth birthday. They were brought by hand from Darantière by the conductor of the Dijon–Paris express. Friends gathered to help Joyce celebrate what was to be from that time forward a triple birthday – his own, that of *The Egoist* serial version of the *Portrait*, and that of the publication of *Ulysses*. With Bloomsday, 2 February has become the great feast-day in the Joycean calendar, celebrated, only half-humorously, in Helsinki and Tokyo as in Dublin and New York.

Writers, reviewers, friends and critics immediately commended or condemned *Ulysses*. Some saw it as a Swiftian satire of modern life in which a modern Ulysses and his Penelope were held up to scorn. Others saw it as an obscene joke. Valery Larbaud, the most influential critic in Paris, wrote: 'With *Ulysses* Ireland makes a sensational return into the best European literature.' Eliot said that 'manipulating a continuous parallel between contemporaneity and antiquity' had 'the importance of a scientific discovery', and he acknowledged its influence on the writing of *The Waste Land*. Virginia Woolf

Sylvia Beach and Joyce in Shakespeare and Company.

thought it 'the book of a self-taught working man'. George Moore saw Joyce as 'a sort of Zola gone to seed'. Paul Claudel returned an autographed copy, but Hemingway said that 'Joyce has a most goddamn wonderful book' and soon smuggled copies, secreted in his trousers, into Detroit from Canada. Yeats, Shaw and John Joyce were among the Irishmen who could not finish the book any more than Nora could. Joyce's Aunt Josephine Murray kept her copy locked up, telling her daughter Kathleen, who passed it on to Joyce, that it was not fit to read. 'If *Ulysses* isn't fit to read,' Joyce answered, 'life isn't fit to live.' But even Stanislaus sent Joyce the praise of a Scotch reviewer from Trieste.

Eye Troubles   During the year following the publication of *Ulysses*, Joyce's eye troubles worsened; he suffered from iritis, acute conjunctivitis and incipient glaucoma. On the recommendation of his doctors he had his teeth, long decayed, extracted. By June 1923, he had had three eye operations, including two iridectomies on his left eye, and by November 1925 he had had a total of eight operations. To recover from the third, he went to Saint-Malo on the English Channel, and he took other trips during the next few years – to Carnac, Arcachon, Ostend, Waterloo, Salzburg, Nice and elsewhere – finding on each journey something necessary to the book that was to follow *Ulysses*. In 1922 Nora and the children visited Ireland ('her native dunghill', Joyce called it in a letter to his Aunt Josephine), where they were forced to flee Galway in a railway carriage that was fired on by both the Irish Republican Army and the Free State troops.

Partly because of his bad eyes, Joyce wrote nothing in the year after *Ulysses* was published, though when he met the generous Miss Weaver for the first time in London, he told her he planned to write 'a history of the world'. And then,

Nora Joyce in Paris in the 1920s. 'I would go anywhere in the world if I could be sure that I could be alone with your dear self without family and without friends.' (*Letters*)

Joyce recuperating after ▶ an eye operation in the 1920s.

in March 1923, he began that vast 'millwheeling vicociclometer' which would be published in 1939 as *Finnegans Wake*. From the start it was, as he told August Suter, 'like a mountain that I tunnel into from every direction, but I don't know what I will find.' He was to go on tunnelling for sixteen years, publishing bits of his 'Work in Progress' in periodicals and as limited editions. Not only a history of Ireland and of the world, it became also a universal mythology, geography, hagiography, psychology and anthropology – a plenitude of paradigms of the lives of Everyman, Everywoman, their children, ancestors, friends and enemies; their falls from grace, their journeys through dreamlands of past and present to encounter battles and loves and trials and crucifixions and dismemberments and resurrections, both 'before and after the Flood'. For the new book discovered by the worthy pioneer was the book of the night as *Ulysses* had been the book of the day. It is Finn Macool lying beside the Liffey, his head at Howth, his feet in Phoenix Park, his wife beside him, watching the microcosmic 'fluid succession of presents' go by like a river of life. It is the story of Tim Finnegan, the whisky-drinking hod-carrier of the ballad, who dies from a

'Finnegans Wake'

^ of a once wallstrait oldparr
is retaled early in bed and later on life down
through all christian minstrelsy. The great
fall of the offwall entailed at such short
notice the schute of Finnegan erse
solid man, that the humptyhillhead of
himself prumptly sends an
unquiring one well to the west in
quest of his tumptytumtoes: and
their upturnpikepointingplace is
at the knock out in the park where
oranges have been laid to rest upon
the green ever and evermore since
Devlins first loved livy.

oystrygods   What clashes here of wills
gaggin   upon wouts, what chance cuddleys,
fishygods   what castles aired T ventilated!
What bidmetoloves sinduced by
what eggtetabsolvers! What
true feeling for their with what
strawng voice of false jiccup!
O here here how hoth sprowled
met the dusk the father of
fornication but, O my
shining stars and body.

Page of the manuscript of *Finnegans Wake*, the book that occupied Joyce from 1923 to 1939.

fall, whose wake becomes a ruction, and who is born again when a noggin of whisky spills on his corpse. In Joyce's illuminated dreambook Finnegan's fall becomes the fall of all men – from Adam to Humpty-Dumpty to Napoleon and Daddy Browning, from the salmon leaps of the Irish rivers to Niagara and the New York stock market of 1929; even to the 'abnihilisation of the etym'. And his rise the same. For if Finn can fall, he can be Finn again, and a book built on a pun (like the Roman Catholic Church, Joyce noted) means 'lots of fun at Finnegan's Wake.'

In several senses *Finnegans Wake* was nothing new for Joyce. Not only is it the night side of the day of *Ulysses* ('the feast is a flyday'); it is also a portrait of the artist as a young man, a middle-aged lecher, a tired old father. It was a continuation of that programme which Joyce announced in the essay 'Portrait' of 1904 – to consider that 'the past assuredly implies a fluid succession of presents'. Like Joyce's other books, it was written on 'the only foolscap available, his own body'. Joyce was again going forth to encounter the reality of experience. But now the experience had grown to embrace all existence, and the words forged in the smithy to name that experience and thereby to 'place it' were fashioned from all languages. 'Je suis au bout de l'anglais,' Joyce told August Suter. And having come to the end of English, he borrowed from Latin, Italian, German, French, Norwegian and many other languages, punning in all of them, even in Finnish and colloquial Arabic. It was 'a jetsam litterage of convolvuli of times lost or strayed, of lands derelict and of tongues laggin too'.

Fragments of the *Work in Progress* were published in *transition*, an international journal edited by Joyce's friends Eugene and Maria Jolas; in the *Transatlantic Review*, edited by Ford Madox Ford; and in limited editions in the United States to protect the copyright. The protection was sorely needed because of the pirating of *Ulysses* in New York by Samuel Roth, who printed a badly mutilated version as a serial in *Two Worlds Monthly*. The piracy was contested in the courts and a protest was lodged, at Joyce's instigation (on his birthday in 1927), by 167 famous persons, including Benedetto Croce, Albert Einstein, T.S. Eliot, E.M.Forster, Giovanni Gentile, André Gide, Ramón Gomez de la Serna, Lady Gregory, Ernest Hemingway, Hugo von Hofmannsthal, D.H. Lawrence, Maurice Maeterlinck, Sean O'Casey, Luigi Pirandello, Miguel de Unamuno, Paul Valéry, Virginia Woolf and W.B.Yeats. The unprecedented publicity relating to this protest may have helped Joyce, but had little effect on Roth, who did not suspend publication until October 1927; he was not finally enjoined from further piracy of *Ulysses* until 28 December 1928.

Meanwhile, Ezra Pound, Miss Weaver and others had cooled to Joyce's new work. Pound called it 'circumambient peripherization', Miss Weaver a 'Wholesale Safety Pun Factory', and Stanislaus a 'drivelling rigamarole' and possibly 'the witless wandering of literature before its final extinction'. Stanislaus demanded Joyce's regression to earlier forms and attitudes. 'Why are you still intelligible and sincere in verse?' he asked, adding that 'Your temperament, like Catholic morality, is predominantly sexual.' He tempered his criticism by relenting in his earlier strictures on *Ulysses*, though this fitted into his argument for a return to earlier modes.

Joyce's faith in his own designs was enough shaken by the criticisms of those who had been closest to his development as an artist to make him demand reassurance from other friends. To one he acknowledged the similarities between his imaginative reconstructions of the world and the psychotic reorganizations of schizophrenia: 'Perhaps it is insanity. One will be able to judge in a century.' But he was certain of one thing – he had to go on digging his tunnel into the mountain of human experience with the new tools of 'monomyth' and paradigmatic language which throughout his career he had been gradually discovering. After having been on the job for twenty years he knew that man's endeavour was all 'play' – the making of matrices or 'mayas' to graph the dream of Brahma called 'reality' while waiting for Godot. As he wrote to Miss Weaver on 16 October 1924, 'I know it is no more than a game, but it is a game that I have learned to play in my own way. Children may just as well play as not. The ogre will come in any case.' Set down in their Sahara, men must, of course, make the map according to their lights and instruments in order to preserve their integrity. Joyce had journeyed from the life-denying delusions of Irish Catholicism, through the transformations of the affirmation of life to the position where all was one – where, though good and evil were not the same, they were both aspects of his lord, who had become the sacramental, monomythic design of all the 'reality of experience'.

Poetry However, partly to show Pound and the rest of the world the essential simplicity of one part of his nature ('the sensitive', as Pound had acutely called it), Joyce got Shakespeare and Company to publish *Pomes Penyeach*, made up of the dozen poems which he had written since the publication of *Chamber Music*, with one left over from the earlier book which he called 'Tilly', Dublinese for the 'extra measure' in his baker's dozen of French-Irish-potatoes-apples. The later poems represent no advance over the earlier, and 'Tilly' – employing the deeply evocative archetypal image of a 'torn bough' as a mannerist shift from a naturalistic image of a drover homing his cows – remains the best:

> He travels after a winter sun,
> Urging the cattle along a cold red road,
> Calling to them, a voice they know,
> He drives his beasts above Cabra.

The voice tells them home is warm.
They moo and make brute music with their hoofs.
He drives them with a flowering branch before him,
Smoke pluming their foreheads.

Boor, bond of the herd,
Tonight stretch full by the fire!
I bleed by the black stream
For my torn bough.

Some of the new poems, too, seemed to be torn things, plucked unformed from Joyce's psyche. They present unrelieved and unelaborated the pain from which his humour and fantastic embroidery of pattern, rhythm, sound and meaning 'protected' him in the prose works. His 'Prayer', for example, written in 1924, ends:

                    I hear
From far her low word breathe on my breaking brain.
Come! I yield. Bend deeper upon me! I am here.
Subduer, do not leave me! Only joy, only anguish,
Take me, save me, soothe me, O spare me!

It was not until John Joyce had died and Giorgio's marriage to Helen Kastor Fleischman had issued, on 15 February 1932, in a grandson named Stephen

Stephen, Joyce's grandson.

James, that Joyce was able again to achieve a poem of completely controlled passion to rank with 'I hear an army' and 'Tilly' – not this time a stilled image of horror, but an image of reconciliation with his own father, his son, his grandson, and, to a certain extent, with himself:

Ecce Puer

Of the dark past
A child is born;
With joy and grief
My heart is torn.

Calm in his cradle
The living lies.
May love and mercy
Unclose his eyes.

Young life is breathed
On the glass;
The world that was not
Comes to pass.

A child is sleeping:
An old man gone.
O, father forsaken,
Forgive your son!

In spite of frequent surgery by Dr Louis Borsch, Dr Alfred Vogt and other ophthalmologists in Paris and Zürich, Joyce's eyes deteriorated until he was nearly blind. But he found time and energy to give new leases to the literary lives of two minor writers – Édouard Dujardin, whose *Les Lauriers sont coupés* he credited with teaching him the technique of the *monologue intérieur* (or stream of consciousness, as William James had called it in the 1890s), and Ettore Schmitz ('Italo Svevo'), his Triestine friend, whose *La Coscienza di Zeno*, an autobiographical novel about a man desperately trying to give up cigarettes, Joyce successfully touted to Larbaud, Adrienne Monnier and others. During the 1930s he would again exert his considerable talents for publicity on behalf of John Sullivan, a tenor whose voice he admired beyond all others.

Joyce was now famous, a man whose works were translated or in the process of being translated into French, German, Italian and other European languages; who knew everyone (Mr and Mrs Archibald MacLeish, Harry and Caresse

The Joyce family, with two friends, in
Zürich after Joyce's operation for cataract
in 1930. It was his ninth operation, and
not the last.

Joyce and Nora in Zürich, 1930.

Crosby, William Carlos Williams, James Stephens, Mr and Mrs Stuart Gilbert, young Samuel Beckett and many others had been added to the intimate circle); and whose name was frequently in the Press. A young Dubliner, Patrick Tuohy, painted his portrait and Brancusi made several sketches for a frontispiece to be used in the Black Sun Press edition of *Tales Told of Shem and Shaun*. C. K. Ogden, hunting the meaning of meaning, translated 'Anna Livia Plurabelle' into Basic English and made Joyce record the original for the Orthological Institute. By 1930 Herbert Gorman had been selected to write his biography. And as early as 1928, two American publishers had offered $11,000 advance and twenty per cent royalties for *Finnegans Wake*, though it was still ten years from completion.

James Stephens, Joyce and the tenor John Sullivan in Paris.

Nevertheless, Joyce's life had become a burden to him. He became increasingly laconic and was given to long silences which seemed to stem, as one friend said, from a 'profound weariness of spirit'. He sighed a great deal and spoke of the 'enormous expense of spirit' which he paid for the comedy of *Finnegans Wake*.

In 1931 the family made what Joyce called their 'fifth hegira', moving to *Family Problems* England, where they settled in May for an indefinite stay at 28b Campden Grove, Kensington. Again one of Joyce's motives for the move was to be nearer to his failing father. Another motive was to marry Nora in order to avoid legal problems with his inheritance. The ceremony was performed in a London registry office on 4 July 1931, a date chosen because it was Joyce's father's

Two 'portraits' of Joyce by Brancusi.

birthday and the marriage served as symbolic penance for the common-law arrangement – of which his father had never approved – under which Joyce and Nora had lived together since 1904, as well as for Joyce's failure to visit his father over the past eleven years. John Joyce died on 29 December 1931, the fifteenth anniversary of the publication of the *Portrait*. That he had borne no resentment and had continued to look on his first son as his favourite is suggested by the adulatory tone of his letters to him and by his making Joyce his only heir; when the will was probated Joyce received property worth the surprising sum of £665 9s. od.

The marriage, which gave Nora a new edge in her natural competition with Lucia for Joyce's affections, also helped to precipitate the girl's mental illness. This gradually assumed the character of extreme hostility to Nora, including violent acts, exaggerated affection for Joyce, and unusual self-consciousness about two physical defects – a slight strabismus and a small scar on her chin; for the scar she repeatedly demanded plastic surgery, only to refuse it later. During the following years, Lucia became increasingly blunt in expressing her opinions, including her own diagnosis of her ailment – that she was 'sex-starved'. Periods of catatonic apathy and inability to concentrate alternated with panic, occasional hysteria and violence. When in December 1933 Joyce was informed by telephone of the success of Morris L. Ernst's argument before Judge John M. Woolsey in New York against the obscenity charges levelled at *Ulysses*, Lucia cut the telephone wires. Several times she ran away from home and later from the private sanatoria where she had to be confined; on one occasion she set fire to her room because, as she later explained, her father's complexion was very red.

Although Lucia's growing madness troubled Joyce deeply and increased his own tendency to hypochondria, insomnia, fits of dark depression and fainting, he both acknowledged and rejected it. During the 1930s he took her from physician to physician, Carl Jung among them. But by and large he saw her affliction as temporary nervousness or an 'inferiority complex' from which she might be rescued by expensive gifts, a change of scene, creative success, or marriage. He set about providing all but the last of these, and for a while even marriage seemed possible. He allowed her to visit Miss Weaver in London and his sister Eileen in Bray. Samuel Beckett and others escorted her but could not love her. Maria Jolas and Mary Colum helped from time to time to take care of her.

Joyce arranged without her knowledge to have her *lettrines* published at his expense in *A Chaucer ABC* and in his own *Pomes Penyeach*. He insisted that her aberrations were brilliance, her dissociation clairvoyance. Able to follow her wild words when others could not, he told Miss Weaver: 'her mind

Joyce and Lucia at Lake Constance, 1932; and the title-page of *Pomes Penyeach*, in Joyce's handwriting and decorated by Lucia. ▶

120

Pomes Penyeach

by

James Joyce

Initial Letters Designed and Illuminated by

Lucia Joyce

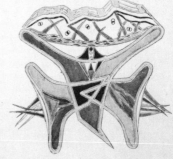

The Obelisk Press
Paris
Desmond Harmsworth Ltd
London

1932

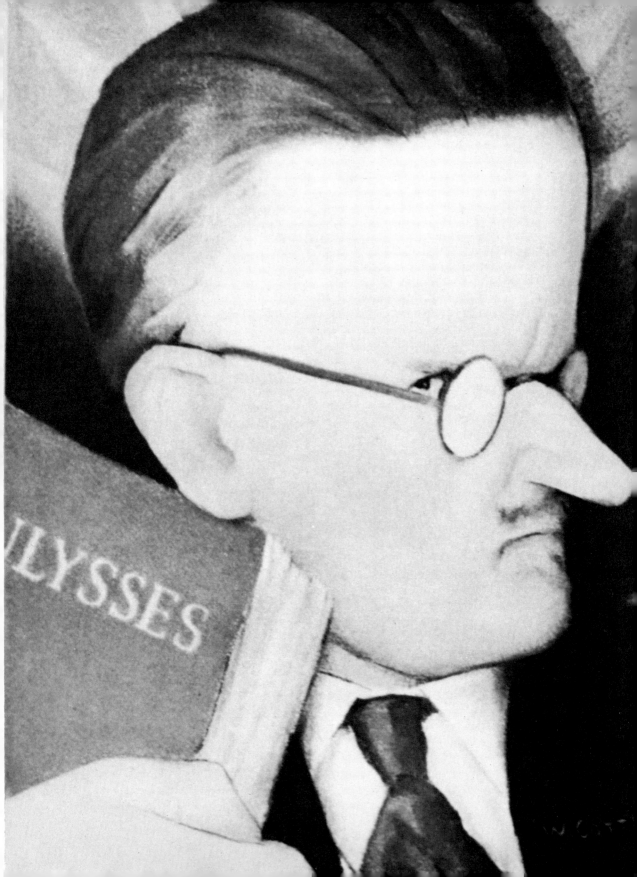

Caricature of Joyce by
W. Cotton, 1934. '. . . the
shuddersome spectacle of this
semidemented zany amid the
inspissated grime of his
glaucous den making believe to
read his usylessly unreadable
Blue Book of Eccles. . . .'
(*Finnegans Wake*)

Joyce with Paul Léon in
Paris, 1936.

is as clear and unsparing as the lightning.' Paul Léon, who for many years
acted as Joyce's secretary, pointed out that 'Mr Joyce trusts one person alone,
and this person is Lucia.'

Joyce was defending Lucia as if it were himself who was being threatened,
as in a sense, of course, it was. Their psyches were strangely alike, even in some
of their deviations from the 'normal', at the same time as they were radically
different. As Jung put it, they were both going to the bottom of a river, but
Lucia was falling and Joyce was diving. What might seem to many to be
'mental abnormality' in Joyce's writings, Jung said in 1932, 'may also be a kind
of mental health which is inconceivable to the average understanding.'

Fortunately, Joyce was concentrating his inconceivable mental health on
finishing *Finnegans Wake* – the mapping of his last Sahara. He could say to
Samuel Beckett, 'I can justify every line of my book' and 'I can do anything
with language.'

He had in one way gone beyond his life-long compulsive packing of conventional meanings towards the only abstraction he allowed himself – the rhythmic shape of phrase, sentence and book. Nino Frank, during their consultations about his Italian translation of 'Anna Livia Plurabelle', was surprised to find him more faithful to sound and rhythm than to sense. To Lucia, Joyce wrote: 'Heaven knows what my prose means. But it's pleasing to the ear. And your designs are pleasing to the eye. That's enough, it seems to me.'

In the autumn of 1938, having taken time off for a rare political action in helping Jewish acquaintances to leave Hitler-occupied territory, Joyce finished his 'maledetto' book. It was an ending which encompassed the endings of his three earlier prose works and brought him back to the beginning. The Liffey flowing into the Irish Sea is Gabriel Conroy accepting death, Stephen Dedalus embracing life and spiritual sonship, Molly Bloom whispering a sleepy 'yes'. Lament for the deaths of friends, elegy for the death of his father and of his daughter's mind, plea for connection and understanding, the passage is at once bitter rejection and compassionate acceptance of the sacramental universe and the ever-present past returning:

O bitter ending! I'll slip away before they're up. They'll never see. Nor know. Nor miss me. And it's old and old it's sad and old it's sad and weary I go back to you, my cold father, my cold mad father, my cold mad feary father, till the near sight of the mere size of him, the moyles and moyles of it, moananoaning, makes me seasilt saltsick and I rush, my only, into your arms. I see them rising! Save me from those therrble prongs! Two more. Onetwo moremens more. So. Avelaval. My leaves have drifted from me. All. But one clings still. I'll bear it on me. To remind me of. Lff! So soft this morning, ours. Yes. Carry me along, taddy, like you done through the toy fair! If I seen him bearing down on me now under whitespread wings like he'd come from Arkangels, I sink I'd die down over his feet, humbly dumbly, only to washup. Yes, tid. There's where. First. We pass through grass behush the bush to. Whish! A gull. Gulls. Far calls. Coming, far! End here. Us then. Finn, again! Take. Bussoftlhee, mememormee! Till thousendsthee. Lps. The keys to. Given! A way a lone a last a loved a long the

Copies of the book reached Joyce in Paris on his birthday in 1939, and it was officially published by Faber and Faber in London and The Viking Press in New York (the firm Huebsch had joined) on 4 May of that year. It was at this birthday party, Joyce's fifty-seventh, that Nora made one of her more Molly Bloomish comments: 'Well, Jim, I haven't read any of your books but I'll have to some day because they must be good considering how well they sell.'

Joyce and Nora.

Joyce and Helen Fleischman Joyce.

During the spring and summer Hitler's advances in Europe frightened *Second World War* Joyce, as violence always had. He became especially concerned for the safety of Lucia, who had to be transferred from one hospital to another for fear of an invasion. Joyce again took to drinking and spending heavily, telling Beckett, 'We're going downhill fast.' By December 1939, Joyce and Nora had moved to Saint-Gérand-le-Puy, near Vichy. Stephen was already there, in the care of Maria Jolas, who conducted a school for refugee children in a near-by château, and Lucia had been moved to a hospital in Pornichet. Helen, who had also suffered a mental breakdown, was in a hospital in Suresnes. Giorgio, disturbed by Helen's worsening illness, restively returned to Paris.

To Joyce's baffled, impotent depression, deepened by his breaking off another friendship – his ten-year association with Paul Léon – was added the burden of severe stomach pains. His cantankerousness and apathetic silences increased. He was a little revived by the *sisu* of the Finns' stand against the Russians in

November 1939 ('the Finn again wakes') but at Christmas he said as he asked Mrs Jolas to dance, 'Come on, then, you know very well it's the last Christmas.'

It was not, quite, though Joyce's productive life was finished: he had no apparent plans to write another book. Just before Christmas of the following year he managed to move his family to Zürich again, save for Lucia, whose *permis de sortir* had expired, and Helen, whose brother, Robert Kastor, took her back to the United States, where her affliction proved, unlike Lucia's, to be curable.

Death   Joyce was old and sick. In Zürich he collapsed, and an X-ray showed that the stomach pains from which he had been suffering were caused by an ulcer which had perforated his duodenum. On Saturday, 11 January 1941, he entered the Schwesterhaus vom Roten Kreuz, where an operation was performed which appeared to have been successful. But the next day he became weaker. He was given blood transfusions. On the following Monday, 13 January, at 2.30 a.m., he died. He was buried two days later, on a dark, snowy day, in the Fluntern Cemetery high above metropolitan Zürich and next to the Zoo. Nora said later: 'He was awfully fond of the lions – I like to think of him lying there and listening to them roar.' Since 1951 she has lain there too.

Stanislaus and Helen are dead now; most of Joyce's brothers and sisters are gone; Giorgio has married again; Lucia lives on in a sanatorium; Stephen, who was educated in the United States, has married and lives in France. I once asked one of his English teachers at Phillips Academy in Andover, Massachusetts, whether he was a good writer. 'No,' he replied. 'He's about average. My best writer is a Crane boy – from the plumbing family in Sheboygan.'

In the famous Horatian summary of his father's character Joyce made Stephen Dedalus in the *Portrait* 'enumerate glibly his father's attributes':

> – A medical student, an oarsman, a tenor, an amateur actor, a shouting politician, a small landlord, a small investor, a drinker, a good fellow, a storyteller, somebody's secretary, something in a distillery, a taxgatherer, a bankrupt and at present a praiser of his own past.

The enumeration is made in answer to Cranly's question, 'What was he?' And as Cranly says, 'The distillery is damn good.'

But nobody is likely to serve a similar hit on Joyce's attributes:

> – A compulsive student, a tenor, an amateur actor, a spoiled priest, a middle-class socialist, an exile, a smalltime swindler, a family man, a rebel, a spend-thrift, a drinker, an egoist, a loner, a looker, a cold fish, a complexive martyr hung up on the sacramental universe, a language teacher, a hand-me-down

dandy, something in a bank, a swooning coward, a great writer and through it all an Irishman who never made his first mistake.

It fails to fit. Even Joyce himself could not get the catalogue right, though he tried it many times. But analysis works no better than catalogue – the man eludes it. In his ways as in his works he belies the dialectical categories of literary critic and psychologist alike – the 'biografiend' and the 'grisly old Sykos' who have done their 'bit on alices' with their 'eatupus complex' when they were 'yung and easily freudened'. Joyce put the point more straightforwardly to his friend Francini Bruni in Trieste in 1919: 'Ideas, classifications, political terminologies leave me indifferent; they are things one has passed beyond. Intellectual anarchy, materialism, rationalism – as if they could get a spider out of his web!' Even Nosey Flynn's well-known label for Bloom comes closer to describing Joyce than analysis can: he was a 'cultured allround man'. But ultimately, unable to reach the Pigeon House any other way, Joyce had to write four great books to explain himself and the world to himself. There they stand. They are, as Stephen Dedalus said of his second-hand copy of Horace, 'human pages'.

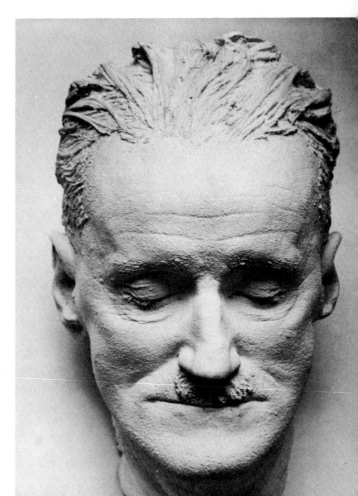

Death mask.
'It's Phoenix, dear.' (*Finnegans Wake*)

Statue of Joyce by Milton Hebald, in the Fluntern Cemetery, Zürich.

1882 James Joyce was born on 2 February in Dublin, the first of ten children. During later life, the only member of his family he remained close to was Stanislaus, born in 1884.

1888 The family moved to Bray. In September Joyce was enrolled in Clongowes Wood College, run by Jesuits.

1891 Joyce wrote *Et Tu, Healy!* (not extant) on the betrayal and death of Parnell. He was withdrawn from Clongowes because of his father's lack of funds.

1892 The family moved to Blackrock.

1893-8 The Joyces, their fortunes declining rapidly, moved to Dublin, where Joyce was enrolled in Belvedere College (also Jesuit). He was an excellent student, winning prizes in national competitions and serving two terms as prefect of the Sodality of the Blessed Virgin Mary. He gradually lost his faith and left the Roman Catholic Church.

1898 Joyce graduated from Belvedere, enrolled in University College, Dublin.

1899 He refused to sign a protest against Yeats's *Countess Cathleen*.

1900 He read 'Drama and Life' before the Literary and Historical Society, published 'Ibsen's New Drama' in the *Fortnightly Review*, and wrote *A Brilliant Career* (a play, not extant) in Mullingar.

1901 He published 'The Day of the Rabblement' (attacking the Irish Literary Theatre) in a pamphlet also containing an essay by F. J. C. Skeffington.

1902 Joyce published 'James Clarence Mangan' in *St Stephen's*, the University College magazine. He graduated from the university with a degree in modern languages. (By this time he had good

beginnings in Italian, French, German and literary Norwegian in addition to Latin.) He left Dublin for Paris to study medicine. Aided by W. B. Yeats and Lady Augusta Gregory, he met some London editors and published two book reviews in the Dublin *Daily Express*.

1903 He published twenty-one book reviews in the *Daily Express*. In April he was called home because his mother was dying: she died in August.

1904 He wrote *A Portrait of the Artist*, an essay-story, on 7 January. He published poems in the *Speaker, Saturday Review, Dana*, and *The Venture*; and stories ('The Sisters', 'Eveline', and 'After the Race') in the *Irish Homestead*, edited by George Russell ('A.E.'). He taught at the Clifton School, Dalkey; sang in the Feis Ceoil, winning the bronze medal; lived in the Martello Tower, Sandymount, with Oliver St John Gogarty; began to write *Stephen Hero*. On 10 June he met Nora Barnacle. In October they travelled to Paris, Zürich, Trieste and Pola, where he began to teach at the Berlitz School.

1905 Joyce and Nora moved to Trieste, where he also taught in the Berlitz School. Their son, Giorgio, was born on 27 July. Joyce submitted *Chamber Music* and *Dubliners* to Grant Richards. His brother Stanislaus joined him in Trieste.

1906 Joyce and his family moved to Rome, where he worked as a foreign correspondent in a bank.

1907 They returned to Trieste. He gave private lessons in English. Elkin Matthews published *Chamber Music*. Joyce wrote articles in Italian for *Il Piccolo della Sera*, a Trieste newspaper. Nora bore his daughter, Lucia, on 26 July.

1909 Joyce visited Ireland. He signed a contract with Maunsel & Co. for the publication of *Dubliners* and returned to Trieste with his sister Eva. He went back to Dublin to organize the Cinematograph Volta. He published two articles, two poems.

1910 He returned to Trieste. The Volta failed. Maunsel & Co. postponed the publication of *Dubliners*.

1912 With his family Joyce made his last trip to Ireland, visiting Galway and Dublin. He published four newspaper articles. The printer destroyed the edition of *Dubliners*. Joyce wrote 'Gas from a Burner'.

1913 He published one poem. Ezra Pound, encouraged by Yeats, wrote to ask for manuscripts.

1914 Dora Marsden (and later Harriet Shaw Weaver) published *A Portrait of the Artist as a Young Man* as a serial in *The Egoist* (London) from 2 February to September 1915, with two *lacunae* caused by Joyce's inability to complete chapter five on the serialization schedule. Grant Richards published *Dubliners*. Joyce began to write *Ulysses* and *Exiles*.

1915 With his family Joyce moved to neutral Zürich, giving his pledge of neutrality to the Austrian authorities. He finished *Exiles*. He was given money from the British Royal Literary Fund at the behest of Pound, Yeats and Edmund Gosse.

1916 He received a grant from the British Treasury Fund. B. W. Huebsch published the *Portrait* in New York.

1917 Joyce received his first gift from Miss Weaver, who eventually was to give him thousands of pounds. He published eight poems in *Poetry* (Chicago). He had his first eye operation and spent three months in Locarno.

1918 He received a monthly allowance from Mrs Harold McCormick. With Claud W. Sykes he organized the English Players. The *Little Review* (New York) serialized *Ulysses* from March 1918 to December 1920. *Exiles* was published by Grant Richards in London and by The Viking Press in New York.

1919 *The Egoist* serialized five instalments of *Ulysses*. Mrs McCormick cut off Joyce's monthly stipend. Joyce and his family returned to Trieste, where he taught in a business school. He published one poem.

1920 He met Pound in Sirmione. Joyce moved with his family to Paris. The *Little Review* was enjoined from publishing *Ulysses* on a complaint by the Society for the Prevention of Vice that it was pornographic.

1921 Joyce agreed to have Sylvia Beach publish *Ulysses* in Paris. Pound, Miss Beach, Adrienne Monnier, Valery Larbaud and others sponsored Joyce's career.

1922 *Ulysses* was published by Miss Beach's Shakespeare and Company on 2 February. Nora and the children visited Galway, where their train was fired on by Civil War troops.

1923 Joyce began to write *Finnegans Wake*. He and his family spent the summer in England.

1924 He published the first fragment of 'Work in Progress' (*Finnegans Wake*) in the *Transatlantic Review* (Paris). He had severe eye trouble, which was to continue for the rest of his life. He visited Brittany and London. Herbert Gorman's biography of Joyce was published by B. W. Huebsch.

1925 Joyce published several fragments of 'Work in Progress'. He visited Fecamp and Arcachon.

1926 Most of *Ulysses* was pirated and serialized in *Two Worlds Monthly* (New York). Joyce published more fragments of 'Work in Progress'. He visited Ostend and Brussels.

1927 Between 1927 and 1938 seventeen instalments of 'Work in Progress' were published in *transition* (Paris) by Eugène Jolas. Many authors and others protested at the piracy of *Ulysses* in New York. Joyce spent nearly three months in London, The Hague and Amsterdam. Shakespeare and Company published *Pomes Penyeach*.

1928 Joyce visited Dieppe, Rouen, Toulon and Salzburg. He published parts of 'Work in Progress' in book form in New York to protect the copyright.

1929 *Ulysse*, the French translation of *Ulysses* was published. Shakespeare and Company published *Our Exagmination round his Factification for Incamination of Work in Progress*. Joyce visited London, Torquay and Bristol.

1930 Stuart Gilbert's *James Joyce's 'Ulysses'* was published. Joyce began his four-year promotion of John Sullivan, the Irish tenor. He underwent more eye surgery, visited England and Wales.

1931 The Joyce family moved to London. Joyce and Nora were married on 4 July. The family returned to Paris in September. Joyce's father died on 29 December. More fragments of 'Work in Progress' were published.

1932 Stephen James Joyce was born on 15 February to Giorgio and Helen Joyce. The poem 'Ecce Puer' written that day, was published in the *New Republic* and reprinted in three other magazines. Lucia had her first breakdown caused by schizophrenia. The family spent the summer in Zürich, Austria and Nice. Paul Léon became Joyce's secretary.

1933 Lucia was hospitalized in Switzerland. The rest of the family spent the summer on Lake Geneva to be near her. In New York Judge John M. Woolsey ruled that *Ulysses* was not pornographic.

1934 *Ulysses* was published by Random House in New York. Giorgio Joyce and his family moved to New York, where they remained for a year-and-a-half. *James Joyce and the Making of 'Ulysses'*, by Frank Budgen, was published. Joyce and Nora visited Grenoble, Zürich, Monte Carlo and Geneva.

1935 Lucia spent ten months with relatives in Ireland and with Miss Weaver in London, but her illness worsened. Joyce and Nora visited Fontainebleau.

1936 *A Chaucer A.B.C.*, with illuminated initial letters by Lucia Joyce, was published in Paris, and Joyce's *Collected Poems* in New York.

1937 The Joyces visited Zürich and Dieppe. The last 'Work in Progress' fragment to be issued separately, *Storiella as She is Syung*, was published in London.

1938 Joyce completed 'Work in Progress'.

1939 *Finnegans Wake* was published in May by Faber and Faber in London and The Viking Press in New York. The Joyces visited Étretat, Berne and Zürich. When war was declared, they returned to France and stayed at La Baule and then St Gérand-le-Puy (near Vichy) to be close to Lucia's hospital.

1940 A revised edition of Gorman's biography of Joyce was published in New York. The Joyces had to leave France for Zürich without Lucia.

1941 Joyce died on 13 January in Zürich, where he was buried.

ACKNOWLEDGMENTS

Any biography of Joyce, however abbreviated, must rely heavily on Richard Ellmann's standard work *James Joyce,* published in 1959.

C. G. A.

This book is published with the approval of the Society of Authors as literary representative of the Estate of James Joyce. Quotations from the works of James Joyce are by permission of the following: Society of Authors and The Viking Press (*Finnegans Wake, Pomes Penyeach*), Jonathan Cape Ltd and The Viking Press (*Dubliners, Chamber Music, A Portrait of the Artist as a Young Man*), The Bodley Head and Random House, Inc. (*Ulysses*), Faber & Faber Ltd and The Viking Press (*The Letters of James Joyce, The Critical Writings of James Joyce*).

BIBLIOGRAPHICAL NOTES

[*Et Tu, Healy!*, Dublin, 1891 or 1892.]

The Holy Office, Trieste, 1905.

Chamber Music, London: Elkin Mathews, 1907.

Gas from a Burner, Trieste, 1912.

Dubliners, London: Grant Richards, 1914.

A Portrait of the Artist as a Young Man, New York: B. W. Huebsch, 1916.

Exiles, London: Grant Richards, 1918.

Ulysses, Paris: Shakespeare & Co., 1922.

Pomes Penyeach, Paris: Shakespeare & Co., 1927

Work in Progress, (published in parts), New York, London, and Paris, 1928–1937.

Collected Poems, New York: The Black Sun Press, 1936.

Finnegans Wake, London: Faber and Faber; New York: The Viking Press, 1939.

Stephen Hero, London: Jonathan Cape; Norfolk, Conn.: New Directions, 1944, rev. ed., 1963.

Epiphanies, Buffalo, New York: Lockwood Memorial Library, University of Buffalo, 1956. Edited by O. A. Silverman.

Works by Joyce

Except for *Et Tu, Healy!* all of Joyce's works listed above are currently available in Britain and The United States from Faber and Faber, Jonathan Cape, Bodley Head, The Viking Press, Random House, or New Directions.

Frank Budgen, *James Joyce and the Making of 'Ulysses'*, Bloomington, Ind., 1960.

Richard Ellmann, *James Joyce*, New York, 1959.

Herbert Gorman, *James Joyce*, New York, 1941.

Stanislaus Joyce, *My Brother's Keeper: James Joyce's Early Years*, New York, 1958.

Kevin Sullivan, *Joyce Among the Jesuits*, New York, 1958.

Works about Joyce: Biographical

Chester G. Anderson (comp.), *Word Index to Stephen Hero*, Ridgebury, Conn., 1958.

—— (ed.), *Joyce's 'A Portrait of the Artist as a Young Man'*, New York (Viking Critical Editions), 1967.

James S. Atherton, *The Books at the Wake: A Study of Literary Allusions in James Joyce's 'Finnegans Wake'*, New York, 1960.

Samuel Beckett and others, *Our Exagmination Round His Factification for Incamination of Work in Progress*, Norfolk, Conn., 1939; rev. ed., 1962.

Joseph Campbell and Henry Morton Robinson, *A Skeleton Key to 'Finnegans Wake'*, New York, 1944.

T. S. Eliot (ed.), *Introducing James Joyce*, London, 1942.

Stuart Gilbert, *James Joyce's 'Ulysses': A Study*, New York, 1930.

Adaline Glasheen, *A Second Census of 'Finnegans Wake'*, Evanston, Ill., 1963.

Miles L. Hanley (comp.), *A Word Index to James Joyce's 'Ulysses'*, Madison, Wis., 1937.

Richard M. Kain, *Fabulous Voyager: James Joyce's 'Ulysses'*, Chicago, Ill., 1947.

Harry Levin, *James Joyce: A Critical Introduction*, Norfolk, Conn., 1941; rev. ed., 1960.

Marvin Magalaner and Richard M. Kain, *Joyce, the Man, the Work, and the Reputation*, New York, 1956.

Joseph Prescott, *Exploring James Joyce*, Carbondale, Ill., 1964.

Robert Scholes and Richard M. Kain, *The Workshop of Daedalus*, Evanston, Ill., 1965.

John J. Slocum and Herbert Cahoon, *A Bibliography of James Joyce, 1882–1941*, New Haven, Conn., 1953.

William York Tindall, *A Reader's Guide to James Joyce*, New York, 1959.

Edmund Wilson, *Axel's Castle: A Study in the Imaginative Literature of 1870–1930*, N.Y., 1931.

Works about Joyce: Critical and Bibliographical

NOTES ON THE PICTURES

21 MAP OF DUBLIN. Drawn by Mrs Hanni Bailey

22 MILLBOURNE LANE, Drumcondra (now Millbourne Avenue). When the Joyce family lived here these were the only houses in the lane, which became an avenue when the 'Corporation' houses were erected beyond its far end. The Dublin Corporation development contains a Joyce Road, but not, apparently, named after James. *Photo the author*

THE TOLKA RIVER is a sad shallow stream, full of debris. Joyce lived near it both in Millbourne Lane and in Richmond Avenue. *Photo the author*

23 JOYCE'S HOME AT 29 WINDSOR AVENUE, Fairview. *Photo the author*

JOYCE'S HOME AT 8 ROYAL TERRACE (now Inverness Road). The Joyce family lived in fourteen homes between the birth of James and his departure for the Continent. *Photo the author*

25 UNIVERSITY COLLEGE, St Stephen's Green, Dublin, the eighteenth-century home of 'Burnchapel' Whaley. University College was founded in 1853 as the Catholic University, at the instigation of Cardinal Newman. It struggled to exist, almost fundless, until the Jesuits took it over in 1883, but even then it stood second to Trinity College. Croessmann Collection, University of Southern Illinois Library.

26 HENRIK IBSEN. Lithograph by Edvard Munch, 1902, after the portrait by Munch of 1896. *Photo Oslo Kommunis Kunstsamlinger, Munch Museum*

27 'IBSEN'S NEW DRAMA'. A reprint of Joyce's article on Ibsen from *The Fortnightly Review*, London, 1900. By courtesy of the Trustees of the British Museum. *Photo Freeman*

28 JOYCE, GEORGE CLANCY ('Davin') AND J. F. BYRNE. Clancy was the only one of Joyce's friends to call him by his first name at University College. After organizing Gaelic League classes in Irish there, and participating in hurley under the auspices of the nationalistic Gaelic Athletic Association, he went on to become mayor of Limerick, where he was murdered by the Black and Tans. Byrne lives on in Brooklyn. Croessmann Collection, University of Southern Illinois Library.

29 FIREPLACE IN THE PHYSICS THEATRE, University College. The old physics theatre is no longer used for classes, and is opened only occasionally for receptions and official functions. The 'dean of studies', Father John Darlington, was Joyce's English teacher for a while, as was Thomas Arnold, brother of Matthew. *Photo the author*

30 MULLIGAN'S IN POOLBEG STREET is the spit and image today of what it was in Joyce's time. *Photo the author*

STATUE OF THOMAS MOORE. Still raising his finger in the street before 'the grey block of Trinity . . . set heavily in the city's ignorance like a great dull stone set in a cumbrous ring', Moore's likeness remains an object of amusement to Dubliners. 'They did right to put him up over a urinal: meeting of the waters,' thinks Bloom, referring to Moore's poem on the Avon and Avoca rivers. Lawrence Collection, National Library of Ireland

THE EXAMINATION HALL, TRINITY COLLEGE, Dublin. *Photo Edwin Smith*

O'CONNELL BRIDGE at Hopkins' Corner, with statues of O'Connell, Gray and Nelson. The view is from Astons Quay (not far from George Webb's bookshop), looking northwest towards Hopkins' Corner at Eden Quay and O'Connell Street. The last door to the right on Eden Quay is Mooney's *sur mer*, where Lenehan 'quaffed the nectar bowl' with Dedalus. Emma Clery may get her name in part from Clery's department store, the large building to the right of Nelson's Pillar. Lawrence Collection, National Library of Ireland

31 ST STEPHEN'S GREEN, looking west towards Grafton Street. The Shelbourne Hotel is out of sight to the right, University College to the left. The pillared building in mid-block beyond the Green is the College of Surgeons, attended for a while, according to *Stephen Hero*, by Lynch. Lawrence Collection, National Library of Ireland

GRAFTON STREET. At the head of this street the slab was set in 1898 for the memorial to Wolfe Tone, never built. Lawrence Collection, National Library of Ireland

32 MAX BEERBOHM, 'Henrik Ibsen, receiving Mr William Archer in audience', *c.* 1900. Municipal Gallery of Modern Art, Dublin

ELEONORA DUSE. *Photo Radio Times Hulton Picture Library*

33 GEORGE RUSSELL (AE), editor of the *Irish Homestead*. Portrait by Count Casimir Markievicz. Municipal Gallery of Modern Art, Dublin. *Photo Barry Mason*

LADY GREGORY. Portrait by Flora Lion, 1913. National Portrait Gallery, London

W. B. YEATS. Portrait by Rothenstein, 1898. Collection Municipal Gallery of Modern Art, Dublin. *Photo Barry Mason*

35 JOYCE IN GRADUATION ROBES. Joyce posed for this picture on 31 October 1902, when he was twenty. Croessmann Collection, University of Southern Illinois Library

GRADUATION GROUP, UNIVERSITY COLLEGE. By the time he graduated Joyce had translated and written many poems and several plays, composed most of his epiphanies, published his essays on Ibsen and Mangan, lectured on 'Drama and Life', and begun to shape the aesthetic questions and definitions which were to occupy his attention in Paris and Trieste. Croessmann Collection, University of Southern Illinois Library

36 THE RIVER LIFFEY, from the North

Wall where Eveline, in the story named after her, could not board the black mass of her ship. Joyce did so, however, each time he left Dublin. *Photo Radio Times Hulton Picture Library*

ARTHUR W. SYMONS. Portrait by Rudolf Helmut Sauter, 1935. National Portrait Gallery, London

37 FOOT OF THE EIFFEL TOWER, Paris. *Photo Courtauld Institute*

38-9 POSTCARD FROM JOYCE TO J. F. BYRNE, from Paris in 1902. Joyce sent two other copies of this photo-postcard to Dublin in December—one in plain English to his family asking for money, and one in dog-Latin to Cosgrave discussing Paris whores. By courtesy of the Beinecke Rare Book and Manuscript Library, Yale University

40 AU SALON, RUE DES MOULINS, 1895. Painting by Henri de Toulouse-Lautrec. Toulouse-Lautrec Museum, Albi

41 READING ROOM, NATIONAL LIBRARY, Dublin. Now, as in 1904, the lights are turned on from the main desk just as the first reader's nose hits the page in the gloom. Here Stephen, with assistance from St Ignatius, Drummond of Hawthornden and others, unfolds the mysteries of Shakespeare, and of himself. *Photo the author*

42 BIBLIOTHÈQUE NATIONALE, Paris, Reading Room. *Photo Roger-Viollet*

43 THE BIBLIOTHÈQUE SAINTE-GENEVIÈVE, Paris, Reading Room. In the winter of 1903 Joyce spent his days in the Bibliothèque Nationale reading Ben Jonson to polish his writing techniques, his nights in the Bibliothèque Sainte-Geneviève, reading Aristotle. *Photo Courtauld Institute*

ENTRANCE TO THE BIBLIOTHÈQUE NATIONALE, Rue Richelieu, Paris. *Photo Roger-Viollet*

THE BIBLIOTHÈQUE SAINTE-GENEVIÈVE, exterior. *Photo Roger-Viollet*

45 O'MEARA'S IRISH HOUSE, on the corner of Wood Quay, Dublin. *Photo Edwin Smith*

47 THE GRAND CANAL from the Baggot Street Bridge towards Charlemont Mall. As Stephen, walking along the canal bank after leaving Emma, nears the bridge, he meets a prostitute, and still humming the chant of the Passion, he transfers his coins into her hand (*Stephen Hero*). St Stephen's Green is about four blocks to the right along Baggot Street. Lawrence Collection, National Library of Ireland

DAME STREET. On the right beyond the first tram is Waterhouse's clock, then the stationery shop of Wisdom Hely, for whom Bloom was 'a traveller for blottingpaper' before he became an ad-canvasser. Lawrence Coll., National Library of Ireland

49 NASSAU STREET, where the sign of Harris's, meditated by Bloom, can be seen three doors down from Yeates & Son. Beyond is Jammet's restaurant, hidden by the tram. Trinity College is to the left behind the iron fence. On this street Joyce met Nora on 10 June 1904. Lawrence Collection, National Library of Ireland

50 NORA BARNACLE JOYCE, whose letters were no doubt a primary source for the non-stop monologue of Molly Bloom. Croessmann Collection, University of Southern Illinois Library

51 ONE OF JOYCE'S FIRST LETTERS to Nora, 15 June 1904. Cornell University Library

LETTER FROM NORA TO JOYCE, 16 August 1904. Cornell University Library

53 JOYCE IN 1904. Photograph by Joyce's life-long friend, C.P. Curran. By courtesy of Yale University Library

54 CHAMBER MUSIC. Title page of Joyce's first collection of poems, published 1907. By courtesy of the Trustees of the British Museum. *Photo Freeman*

56 SANDYCOVE. Croessmann Collection, University of Southern Illinois Library

MARTELLO TOWER, SANDYCOVE, Bloomsday 1964. One of the many Martello towers built along the coast to protect Ireland from possible attack by Napoleon, this 'omphalos', as Mulligan calls it, is now a Joyce museum. On the sixtieth anniversary of Bloomsday there were celebrations of *Ulysses* throughout the world, including a pilgrimage to Dublin to the scenes in which Bloom, Stephen and the others are placed. *Photo Irish Times*

58 POLA, ARCH OF SERGIUS, with the Berlitz School to the right. Joyce was apparently embarrassed about his Balkan address and instructed Stanislaus not to give it out without asking his leave. *Photo the author*

2 VIA GIULIA, POLA, where Joyce settled. The Berlitz school was just round the corner. *Photo the author*

7 VIA MEDOLINO, POLA, where Joyce and Nora moved in during the first or second week of 1905. *Photo the author*

59 TEMPLE OF AUGUSTUS and Italian Renaissance house in Pola. *Photo Thames and Hudson archives*

60 POLA HARBOUR AND AMPHITHEATRE. Joyce noticed changes in himself as a married man in 'Siberia': 'My new relation has made me a somewhat grave person and I have got out of the way of dissertations. I drink little or nothing, smoke vastly, sing rarely. I have become very excitable.' (*Letters*)

61 THE GRAND CANAL, TRIESTE. *Photo Mansell Collection*

63 THE BERLITZ SCHOOL, PIAZZA PONTEROSSO, TRIESTE. When they first came to Trieste in 1905, Joyce and Nora lived in the Piazza Ponterosso, on the third floor of the first building to the left of the eventual home of the Berlitz School.

Notes *Page*

At that time the school was still at 32 via San Nicolò. The Joyces moved to 31 via San Nicolò, but the School then moved to the Piazza Ponterosso. *Photos the author*

64 PIAZZA DELLA BORSA, TRIESTE. *Photo Mansell Collection*

65 BULL ALLEY, DUBLIN. Lawrence Collection, National Library of Ireland

THE BANK OF IRELAND moved into Parliament House shortly after it became unnecessary as the seat of government following the Act of Union in 1800. Lawrence Collection, National Library of Ireland

67 EILEEN JOYCE, presumably on the day she was married in Trieste, 1915. Cornell University Library

STANISLAUS JOYCE IN TRIESTE, where his main disappointments can be inferred from his Aunt Josephine's letter to him of 6 June 1906: Nora's laziness and irritability, Jim's drinking and lack of progress in his writing, and what he considered the bad management of the Berlitz School. Lawrence Collection, National Library of Ireland

68 NORA, GIORGIO and MRS ANNE BARNACLE (Nora's mother), Galway, 1912. While Nora and the children were visiting her relatives in Galway, Joyce wrote her complaining letters from Dublin, where he was trying unsuccessfully to persuade George Roberts to publish *Dubliners*, as he had contracted to do. Croessmann Collection, University of Southern Illinois Library

69 JOYCE WITH GIORGIO IN TRIESTE. Croessmann Collection, University of Southern Illinois Library

70 THE OLD ABBEY THEATRE, Dublin. Performance of *The Shewing-Up of Blanco Posnet* by Shaw, 1909. From Raymond Mander and Joe Mitchenson Theatre Collection.

Page

71 THE OLD ABBEY THEATRE, Dublin. Exterior. *Photo Irish Tourist Board*

THE OLD ABBEY THEATRE, Dublin. Interior. *Photo Irish Tourist Board*

SKETCHES OF THE ABBEY THEATRE AUDIENCE from a pamphlet, *The Abbey Row*, 1907, by W.B. Yeats. By courtesy of the Trustees of the British Museum. *Photo Freeman*

72 7 ECCLES STREET, where J.F. Byrne was living when Joyce returned to Dublin for two extended stays in 1909, and later to be the address of Leopold and Molly Bloom (*Ulysses*). The building is now marked for demolition. Painting by Flora H. Mitchell. Croessmann Collection, University of Southern Illinois Library

74 VOLTA THEATRE, 45 MARY STREET. Drawing by A. Brioscu. Croessmann Collection, University of Southern Illinois Library

77 J. M. SYNGE. Portrait from *The Abbey Row*, 1907, following the first performance of his *The Playboy of the Western World* at the Abbey Theatre. By courtesy of the Trustees of the British Museum. *Photo Freeman*

WELLINGTON MONUMENT in Phoenix Park, a testimonial designed by R. Smirke and completed in 1860. *Photo the author*

I. DOWNES'S CAKESHOP is a block east of Nelson's Pillar that was; the location and shop itself are relatively unchanged since Joyce's day. *Photo the author*

78 PIAZZA GIAMBATTISTA VICO, Trieste. Joyce apparently first read Vico's *La Scienza nuova* (1744) when he was in Trieste, and this interest continued for the rest of his life. *Photo the author*

79 EZRA POUND, 1916. From Pound's volume *Lustra*. By courtesy of the Trustees of the British Museum. *Photo Freeman*

81 MICHAEL HEALY, Nora Joyce's uncle.

This postcard photograph was taken by the Empire Studio, 62 Dame Street, Dublin, probably when Healy went to Dublin from Galway in June 1935, to see how Lucia was getting along with her Aunts Eileen and Eva in Bray. *Courtesy of Yale University Library*

82 JOYCE IN ZÜRICH. Croessmann Collection, University of Southern Illinois Library

83 HARRIET SHAW WEAVER. According to Miss Jane Lidderdale, the late Miss Weaver's niece and biographer, this photograph was taken at about the time Miss Weaver was publishing *A Portrait* in *The Egoist*. *Courtesy of Miss Jane Lidderdale. Photo Clareville Studios*

84 SEEFELDSTRASSE, ZÜRICH. *Photo the author*

CAFÉ ODÉON, ZÜRICH, 1915. Interior. *Photo Baugeschichtliches Archives, Zürich*

85 CAFÉ TERRASSE, ZÜRICH, 1915. *Photo Zürich Public Library*

CAFÉ ODÉON, ZÜRICH. Exterior. *Photo Baugeschichtliches Archives, Zürich*

86 PFAUEN HOTEL AND RESTAURANT, ZÜRICH. *Photo Baugeschichtliches Archives, Zürich*

STEFAN ZWEIG. *Photo Staatsbibliothek Berlin Bildarchiv*

FRANK WEDEKIND. *Photo Staatsbibliothek Berlin Bildarchiv*

ROMAIN ROLLAND. *Photo Staatsbibliothek Berlin Bildarchiv*

87 THE JOYCE FAMILY IN ZÜRICH, 1915. This photograph was taken by Ottocaro Weiss in Küsnacht in front of the Gasthaus Zur Sonne. At that time Giorgio was ten years old and Lucia eight. *By courtesy of Yale University Library*

88 JOYCE'S DANCE, by Desmond Harmsworth, 1930s. A sketch of 'Joyce executing a ballet step on the sidewalk at midnight after a richly convivial dinner in his favourite Paris restaurant'. Note by the artist when the sketch appeared on the cover of *The Texas Quarterly*, III, 1960. *By courtesy of the Humanities Research Center, University of Texas*

89 CARICATURE OF JAMES JOYCE, by César Abin. Joyce dictated this caricature in 1932 to the Spanish artist, with details to suggest his posture, comic view of life, near blindness, superstition, dejection, mourning, poverty, romance, and dominion over the earth, which has but a single country, Ireland. *Transition*, no. 21 (March 1932)

90 LOCARNO. *Photo Zürich Public Library*

PENSION DAHEIM, Locarno. *Photo the author*

91 UNIVERSITÄTSSTRASSE, ZÜRICH, where Joyce lived from January to October in 1918. *Photo Fritz Senn*

92 CAFÉ ZIMMERLEUTEN, ZÜRICH, *c.* 1917. *Photo Zürich Public Library*

93 PORTRAIT OF JOYCE by Frank Budgen. Oil. Croessmann Collection, University of Southern Illinois Library (Gift of Charles E. Feinberg)

94 Programme of The English Players' first production at the Pfauen Theater in Zürich. *Photo Zürich Public Library*

95 JOYCE. Photograph taken in Zürich in or before 1918. The dedication is to Paul Ruggiero, dated 8 December 1918

97 ETTORE SCHMITZ (ITALO SVEVO) and his family. *Photo Giornalfoto, Trieste*

99 PHOTOGRAPH OF JOYCE AND SYLVIA BEACH in Paris, 1920. Sylvia Beach published *Ulysses* in 1922 on 2 February, Joyce's birthday, and a date which all his life he surrounded with a cult.

100 CARTOON OF JOYCE AND HIS FRIENDS by F. Scott Fitzgerald. Dated July 1928. Printed in Sylvia Beach, *Shakespeare and Company*, 1959, page 117

101 'THE DUC DE JOYEUX SINGS'. This lampoon on Joyce's assertions of noble ancestry is by Wyndham Lewis, done in the 1920s. Collection Walter Michel

102 LUCIA JOYCE as a child in Zürich. Croessmann Collection, University of Southern Illinois Library

LUCIA JOYCE as a young woman, perhaps during one of the visits of the Joyce family to England in 1930 or 1931. By courtesy of Yale University Library

103 THE JOYCE FAMILY IN PARIS, early 1920s (Lucia, Nora, James, Giorgio). Croessmann Collection, University of Southern Illinois Library

104 FORD MADOX FORD, JOYCE, EZRA POUND AND JOHN QUINN in Pound's Paris studio, 1923

105 JOYCE IN THE 1920S. Joyce bought a second finger-ring as a present to himself following the publication of *Ulysses* in 1922. By courtesy of Yale University Library. *Photo Berenice Abbott*

107 PAGE PROOF OF 'ULYSSES' with Joyce's corrections. By permission of the Society of Authors. By courtesy of the Trustees of the British Museum. *Photo Freeman*

109 SYLVIA BEACH AND JOYCE in Shakespeare and Company. Croessmann Collection, University of Southern Illinois Library

110 NORA BARNACLE JOYCE in Paris in the 1920s. By courtesy of Yale University Library. *Photo Berenice Abbott*

111 JOYCE RECUPERATING AFTER AN EYE OPERATION in the 1920s. By courtesy of Yale University Library

112 PART OF MS OF 'FINNEGANS WAKE'. By permission of the Society of Authors. *Photo by courtesy of the British Museum*

115 STEPHEN, JOYCE'S GRANDSON. Croessmann Collection, University of Southern Illinois Library

117 JOYCE WITH HIS FAMILY and two friends in Zürich, 1930, after his ninth eye operation. *Photo Fritz Senn*

JOYCE AND NORA in Zürich, 1930. This photograph was taken by Joyce's friend, Georges Borach, following his eleventh eye operation in the Clinique de la Croix Rouge, Zürich on 15 May. He was to die in the same hospital ten years later. By courtesy of Yale University Library

118 JAMES STEPHENS, JOYCE AND JOHN SULLIVAN in Paris. Joyce's adulation of the tenor, Sullivan, was unbounded. Croessmann Collection, University of Southern Illinois Library

119 DRAWING OF JOYCE by Constantin Brancusi. The abstract whirl served as the frontispiece of *Tales Told of Shem and Shaun*, 1929

DRAWING OF JOYCE by Brancusi. Collection of Mrs Marcel Duchamp. *Photo Lockwood Memorial Library, State University of New York at Buffalo, N.Y.*

121 JOYCE AND LUCIA at Lake Constance, 1932. Croessmann Collection, University of Southern Illinois Library

TITLE PAGE OF 'POMES PENY-EACH' in Joyce's handwriting. *Pomes Penyeach* was published in Paris in 1932. By permission of the Society of Authors. By courtesy of the Trustees of the British Museum. *Photo Freeman*

122 CARICATURE OF JOYCE by W. Cotton, 1934. Published in colour in *Vanity Fair*, March 1934

INDEX

Page numbers in italics refer to illustrations

DATE DUE

Demco, Inc. 38-293